THE LOST BOOK OF ENOCH

THE LOST BOOK OF ENOCH

David Humphreys

JANUS PUBLISHING COMPANY LTD
Cambridge England

First published in Great Britain 2004 by
Janus Publishing Company Ltd
The Studio
High Green
Great Shelford
Cambridge CB22 5EG

www.Januspublishing.co.uk

Reprinted 2006
Reprinted 2009
Reprinted 2011

British Library Cataloguing-in-Publication Data.
A catalogue record for this book is available from the British Library.

ISBN 978-1-85756-504-1

Cover design Simon Hughes
Based on an idea by the author

Printed and bound in the UK by PublishPoint
from KnowledgePoint Limited, Reading

INTRODUCTION

I came across the mentioning of the Book of Enoch in the New Testament – in fact, in the Letter of St Jude. This aroused my curiosity, but to find a copy, an English translation, was to take me some time.

On a visit to a synagogue with a small group of fellow Christians, I asked about the Book of Enoch. Our guide took us into the library and a large encyclopaedia was taken down and the Book of Enoch was looked up. A translation was made many years ago, but as this book is not acceptable to orthodox Judaism, we were told it was of no importance.

This only made me more determined to find a copy. My search has been very much on a part-time basis, in the belief that if I am meant to discover it the book will come into my hands somehow. I tried local libraries, second-hand bookshops and specialist theological booksellers, but with no success. Then, on a whim, I checked again with my local library service and a copy was now available (it had been with a bookbinder).

So here we are. I hope you will find The Lost Book (The Book of Enoch) as interesting as I have found it to be. I wanted this modern edition to be uncomplicated and available to be read as a book without a load of notes, subtexts and other observations.

The authors of the Book of Enoch commenced their writings about 200 BC and continued up until around AD 100. It was seen originally as one of the most important works of Jewish literature, yet Jewish scholars appear not to acknowledge it as such.

The original text was written in the hope that the combined work would become translated into various languages and, hopefully, become "a source of joy, illumination and much wisdom". The authors' hopes were achieved in the centuries preceding and following the Christian era. During this period the full benefit of the apocalyptic writing became widespread and known to many of the disciples and writers of the New Testament – for example, St Jude and St Barnabas. In their day it had all the weight of a canonical book right up to the fourth century AD. It was then that its authenticity was questioned, and Hilary, Jerome and Augustine later banned the reading of the Book of Enoch.

For whatever reasons, the Book of Enoch soon vanished and was lost to Western Christianity for many centuries. It was only the discovery of an Ethiopic version of the book in the 1800s that led to the long period of translation and further investigation of texts and scripts coming to fruition, and the translation of the Book of Enoch commenced.

The original authors were said to be true successors of the Old Testament prophets. However, then as now, Jewish authorities insisted that the Law was complete, being the highest and final word of God. Earlier scholars believed the Book of Enoch to contain even earlier work, possibly from the Book of Noah, with other text coming from pre-Maccabaean period, consisting of dream visions from the time when Judas Maccabaeus was warring.

The Book of Enoch, like the Book of Daniel, was probably written partly in Aramaic and partly in ancient Hebrew. It is interesting to note that these earlier texts were written in verse.

For the scholarly amongst you, the source I have worked from is the 1912 edition by R H Charles DLitt, DD, Fellow of Merton College and Fellow of the British Academy, published by Oxford, Clarendon Press.

THE LOST BOOK
(The Book of Enoch)

1

The words of the blessing of Enoch, with which he blessed the elect and righteous, who will be living in the day of tribulation, when all the wicked and godless are to be removed. And he took up his parable and said: "I, Enoch, a righteous man, whose eyes were opened by God, saw the vision of the Holy One in the heavens, which the angels have shown me and from them I heard everything. And from them I understood what I saw, but not for this generation but for a remote one which is to come. "Concerning the elect, I took up my parable concerning them and said, "The Holy Great One will come forth from His dwelling and the eternal God will tread upon the earth, even upon Mount Sinai [and appear from His camp] and appear in the strength of His might from the heaven [of heavens]. And all shall be struck with fear, and all shall quake, and great fear and trembling will seize them throughout the world. High mountains shall be shaken and high hills shall become low and melt like wax before a flame.

The earth shall be totally torn and all that live on the earth will perish. There will be a judgement upon all people.

But the righteous people will have nothing to fear; He will make peace with them and will protect them, His elect. His mercy shall be upon them and they shall belong to God. They will prosper and be blessed. He will help them all and Light shall come over them and they will be in His peace.

Behold! He comes with ten thousands of his Holy Ones to bring justice to all people and He will destroy all the ungodly. He will judge and convict all flesh. Of all ungodliness and deeds they have committed and for those things spoken ungodly against Him [i.e., taking His name in vain]."

2
Observe you, everything from the stars and planets, the rising and the setting of the sun and moon, their variations in all seasons of the year. Do not infringe or go beyond such bounds that are set, nor interfere with the balance of their order.

Consider the earth, and pay attention to the things that take place from the greatest to the least. How strong they are and how many things are unmoveable and changeless. Yet all these are but the works of God. Consider the summer time and winter, how the whole earth is filled with water, clouds and dew that rain down on it.

3
Observe the winter time, how all the trees seem as though they have withered and shed all their leaves, except the fourteen types of tree which do not lose their foliage but retain their foliage from two to three years till the new leaves grow.

4
Again, observe the days of summer how the sun is always above you. You seek shade and shelter from the heat of the sun. The ground itself seems to glow and shimmer with the heat. So hot can be the ground that you cannot bear to walk on it or on any rock because it burns your feet with its heat.

5
Observe how the trees cover themselves with green leaves and some bear fruit. Remember and know that these are from God; they are his works. Recognise them as such, that He who lives forever made them all. All His works go on from year to year, forever. And all the tasks, which they accomplish for Him, do not change unless He changes them. Also look at the seas and rivers that do as He commands. But you, you have not stood firm nor carried out the commandments of the Lord, but turned away and spoken with pride and hard words, with impurity of thought and word against His greatness. Oh you hard-hearted people; you will never find true peace.

6

Therefore you will feel disgust and hatefulness for all the days of your life, and your life will perish throughout many long years. This will be multiplied into an eternity of curses. For you, there will be no mercy!

7

In those days your names will be known an eternal disgust to all righteous people. You will lead many to curse and all sinners and godless people shall blame you.

8

All godless people will be cursed.

9

But they that are God-fearing and righteous in His sight shall rejoice and their sins will be forgiven. And there will be every mercy, peace and forbearance; there shall be salvation for them and they will dwell in the Light. Yet, for all of you sinners there shall be no salvation, for you will bear a curse.

For the elect, there shall be light, grace and peace for every one of you, and you shall inherit the earth.

10

To the elect of God shall be given wisdom, for they shall live and never again live to sin. Either through ungodliness or through pride and arrogance. For those who receive wisdom shall become humble.

11

They shall never again trespass against the Lord, neither sin throughout the days of their lives. They will not die of God's anger or wrath but they will live their allotted days of life. They shall live in peace and their lives will be spent in joy, in eternal gladness and eternal peace, all the days of their life.

12
In the earlier days of mankind, many had beautiful daughters. Now there were a group of Angels from the heavenly realms, who saw and lusted after these daughters of mankind, and they spoke to each other.

"Come, let us choose each one of us a wife from amongst these beautiful daughters that they may conceive children to us." Their leader was called Semjaza and he said to the group, "I wonder if any of you will agree to actually doing this, I will have to pay the penalty of such a great sin." The others thought about this and one of them suggested that they all swear an oath to share the penalty and go ahead with the plan. They all agreed. The idea spread and in all two hundred descended (in the days of Jared) to the earth and appeared on Mount Hermon. Apart from Semjaza, there were other leaders – Arakiba, Rameel, Kokabiel, Tamiel, Ramiel, Danel, Ezeqeel, Baraqijal, Asael, Armaros, Batarel, Ananel, Zaqiel, Samsapeel, Satarel, Turel, Jomjael and Sariel. These were their chiefs or leaders of tens.

13
On arrival on the mountain they went their ways and each took a human wife. They had intercourse with them. While they were with their wives they taught them charms and enchantments. They cut the roots of plants and taught them about the plants they collected and used. Each woman became pregnant. Each child born was huge, like a giant in height.

14
As they grew up they wanted more than their share of the things men in those days had acquired and they were becoming a burden on those around them. These giants of men turned against the normal human beings in their midst and destroyed them. Not satisfied with this, they began to have unnatural relationships with not just animals, but with birds, reptiles and fish. Then they had a desire for blood and started to kill one another for they had turned cannibalistic. They did eat human flesh and drink the blood of each other who they had killed.

15
Such evil acts brought hatred by other inhabitants of the earth against these giants.

16
Meanwhile, Azazel had made friends of the humans near his home and he taught them how to make knives and swords, shields and breastplates. He taught them about the different metals in the earth, how to use them and the art of making bracelets, ornaments and weapons. Then he taught others how to adorn themselves and colour their eyelids and the use of precious stones and the making of coloured tinctures.

17
Amongst these people there was great ungodliness and many had sex outside marriage [fornication]. Many were led into this way of life and most became corrupt in so many ways.

18
Semjaza taught the skills of enchantments and the use of roots of plants. Armaros taught the uses of enchantments, Baraqijal taught astrology, Kokabel taught man about the constellations. Ezeqeel spoke about the knowledge of the clouds. Two others gave instruction on the signs of the earth and sun. They were: Araqiel (earth) and Shamsiel (sun). Sariel taught about the course of the moon. Then many men were starting to die and their cries went up to the heavens.

19
In the heavens the angels Michael, Uriel, Raphael and Gabriel looked down and saw the blood of mankind being shed and all the evil and lawlessness that was going on. They said to each other: "The earth once made without inhabitants now cries out to the very gates of heaven! For they cry out, 'To you, the holy ones of heaven, our souls cry out! Bring our cries and calls for help to the Most High'."

20
The angels came to the throne of God on behalf of mankind and they said to the Lord, "Lord of lords, God of gods, King of kings and God of ages. The throne of thy glory stands for all generations and ages; your name is Holy and Glorious and Blessed. You have made all things; you have power over all things. All is naked to your sight; you see all things and nothing is hidden from your sight. Look and see what Azazel has done on earth – he has taught unrighteousness and has revealed eternal secrets that were once the preserve of heaven. Only for men to strive to learn about. Then there is Semjaza; you gave him authority over his associates. In fact all of them have gone and 'slept' with human women and defiled themselves sexually and taught the people all kinds of sins. Each woman has given birth to an oversized child, a giant in stature. Now they have gone wrong and killed many, spilling blood upon the ground, and there is much unrighteousness. Now the souls of mankind who have died cry out to the very gates of heaven, unceasing, due to the lawlessness and evil on the earth. You know all things even before they happen. You see them and know they go on. So far you have not said to us as to what must be done."

21
Then the Lord answered and spoke to Uriel. He told him to go to the son of Lamech (Noah) and to tell him: "Hide yourself! Reveal to him the end that is approaching, that the earth will be destroyed by a deluge. Instruct him that he may escape, that his seed may be preserved for future generations of the world."

Then he spoke to Raphael: "Bind Azazel hand and foot and cast him into the darkness. Make an opening in the desert, which is in Dudael, and cast him into it. Place upon him rough and jagged rocks that will ensure complete darkness. Ensure also that his face is securely covered so he sees no light at all. He will stay there forever but on the day of the great judgement he will be cast into the fire. Then go and heal the earth, which these angels have corrupted; heal them of the plague. Ensure that the children of men do not perish because of all the secret things that have been disclosed to them.

The earth has been corrupted by the teachings of Azazel and he is responsible for all sins."

He then addressed Gabriel: "Proceed against all the bastards, reprobates, the children of fornication. The children of these fallen angels, proceed against them amongst men and set them against each other so that they destroy each other in battles. For their days are few. These children will die but their fathers will plead for them – disregard their requests. They would hope to live an eternal life, which they count as five hundred years."

Then the Lord turned to Michael: "Go and bind Semjaza and his associates, who themselves have taken human wives and defiled themselves and made themselves 'unclean'. When their sons have killed each other, for they will see this happen, bind them fast for seventy generations and place them in the valleys of the earth until the day of their judgement and when they will be consumed. In those days they will be led off to the abyss of fire into a torment and eternal prison forever."

22

"Whosoever shall be condemned and destroyed will be bound together with others, to the end of all generations. All the spirits of reprobates, children of these fallen angels, all who have wronged mankind will be destroyed. Now destroy all wrong from the face of the earth and let every evil deed and work come to an end. Let the plant of righteousness and truth appear and let there be joy evermore!"

23

Then all the righteous people escaped and lived until they had thousands of children. All the days of their youth up to their old age were spent in complete peace. The whole earth was tilled in righteousness; trees were planted and blessed. Desirable trees were planted along with vines. The vines were plentiful and yielded a lot of wine. All seed planted were to yield a thousand-fold and from the olives should have given ten presses full of oil.

24
The Lord God commanded that the earth be cleansed from all oppression, all unrighteousness and from all sin. Any uncleanness found should be destroyed. The children of men shall become righteous and all nations shall offer Him adoration and praise. "All shall worship Me," said the Lord our God. Again He said that the earth shall be cleansed from all defilement, from all sins, from all punishment and torment. Never again would He send the deluge from that generation to future generations of mankind.

25
Before these things had taken place, Enoch was hidden from the children of men. They had no idea where his abode was or what had become of him as his activities had connections with they who were called the Watchers of the Holy Great One (God Almighty). His life had been spent with these holy Ones.

26
Now I, Enoch, was blessing and praising the Lord when the Watchers called me. "Enoch! You, who are a writer of righteousness, go and declare to the Watchers of the Heaven who have now left heaven and the Holy Eternal Place. For they have gone and defiled themselves by having sex with women who they have taken as wives. Say to them: 'You have brought great destruction to the earth. You will have no peace or forgiveness of your sins. For you have enjoyed yourself with your children. For they shall see the destruction of their children and will have much anguish over their deaths. Although you may cry out for mercy, no mercy or peace will you be given.'"

After this Enoch went and found Azazel and said to him, "Azazel, you will not find peace. A severe sentence and charge has been made against you and you will find yourself bound up. There will be no toleration for your actions; you will have no right of appeal because of the unrighteousness that you have taught; the ungodliness and the sinful ways you have taught mankind."

27

I [Enoch] then found the others and they were very much afraid and so fearful that they started to tremble with fear. They asked me to draw up a petition for them to ask for forgiveness and to take it to Almighty God on their behalf. Before, they were able to face Him, but now this was forbidden and, besides, they felt so guilty they couldn't even speak or lift their eyes up towards heaven. I wrote out their petition for them and their prayers with regard to their spirits. Taking into account their individual deeds [sins]; their requests for forgiveness. I wrote this all out for them and left them there. I travelled to Dan [the Land of Dan is south-west of Hermon] and sat there by the waterside. Here I sat quietly, reading through the petition until I fell asleep.

28

Whilst I lay asleep I had a dream – or perhaps visions. These visions were of chastisement and I heard a voice telling me to tell the sons of heaven, to reprimand them. When I woke up I got to my feet and went back to them and found them weeping together in a place called Abelsjail [between Lebanon and Seneser] with their faces covered. I told them of the visions I had whilst asleep and I began to speak the words of the righteous and to reprimand the Heavenly Watchers.

29

There is a book of the words of righteousness, and of the reprimand of the eternal Watchers in accordance with the command of the Holy Great One in that vision. I had seen in my sleep what I can now relate to you in the flesh. This which has been given to man to converse with and to understand with the heart. As He has created and given to man the power of understanding, the word of wisdom. He has also given me the power to reprimand the Watchers, the Children of Heaven.

I told them, who were gathered around me, that it appears that their petition will not be granted to them throughout the period of eternity. Judgement has been passed upon them. They will never ascend back into heaven for all eternity. They are to be bound to the earth for all the days of the world. They shall see the destruction of all their sons and they will cease to have any pleasure in them. Their sons will all die by the sword and their petitions on behalf of their sons has been declined as well.

30

I told them about a further vision I had had. In this vision clouds invited me and a mist called me. Then the course of the stars and lightnings brought me quickly with the winds. All this brought me up to heaven. I walked toward a wall built of crystals and surrounded by tongues of fire. This frightened me very much. Yet I went into the tongues of fire and came to a large house, which also was built of crystals. The walls of this house were like a tessellated [regularly chequered cubed blocks like in a mosaic] floor of crystals and so was the groundwork. The ceiling of the house was like the path of the stars and the lightnings. Between them were fiery Cherubim, their heaven like clear water. A flaming fire surrounded the walls and its very portals blazed with fire. I entered the house and it was hot as fire and yet cold as ice. There were no delights that you would find in a normal house. I started to tremble with fear to such an extent that I fell over and landed face down. I had another vision come to me.

31

There before me was another house, greater than the first. It was open to me but was built of flames of fire. It was so splendid and magnificent that words fail me to describe it to you. Even the floors were of flame and above me were lightnings and even the path of the stars was seen. Yet the very ceiling appeared to be made of flaming fire. As I peered further into this house there was a high throne with the appearance of crystal and wheels. It had wheels like bright sunlight and I could see Cherubim. From underneath this throne came streams of even more fire and it was impossible to look further at it. Great Glory seemed to be seated upon this throne; the very living God, God Almighty, and His clothing shone brighter than the sun and were whiter than snow. So magnificent was He, that not even the angels of heaven could look at Him. Still more fire surrounded

Him and a great fire was before Him and no one could come near to the Lord. As I looked on I saw what must be over a million persons standing before the throne. There was no sign of anyone acting as a counsellor to Him.

32

The most Holy of these persons were always with Him; they never left his sight. I was to be found still on my face on the ground. Then He called to me and said, "Come here, Enoch, and hear what I have to say!" I was now rising to my feet and one of the Holy Ones came to me and helped me rise up and enter this house. I felt I had to bow my head and also because of the brightness of His Glory. He then spoke to me again.

33

"Fear not, Enoch. You are a righteous man and the writer of righteousness. Come closer and listen to me. Go, and say to the Watchers of Heaven, those who have asked you to intercede on their behalf, and tell them this: 'You should intercede for men, not men for you! You have left the high and holy heaven and have had a relationship with women and defiled yourself with the daughters of men. You have taken wives and carried on like the children of earth, and the outcome has been the birth of giants – your sons! You were holy, spiritual, living the eternal life, but you defiled yourselves with the blood of women and now have children with the blood of flesh. Acting like children of men who have lusted after the flesh and blood, like mortal men who do such things only to perish and die.

"'Of men, I have given them wives that they may impregnate and give birth to children and that they may have what they need on earth. But you! You were formerly spiritual, living the eternal life of immortality for all the generations of the world. Being in this state you are not given wives nor anyone in heaven as this was your dwelling place.'

34

"Now there are giants who are the product of the spirits and the flesh and they shall be known as evil spirits upon the earth and the earth shall be their dwelling place. Evil spirits have proceeded from their bodies because they were born from mankind and from Holy Watchers their primal origin. Therefore they shall be evil spirits on earth and evil spirits they shall be called.

"The spirits of heaven shall belong to heaven and the spirits of the earth shall belong to the earth. As for the spirits of the giants, they afflict, oppress, destroy, attack, do battles and work destruction on the earth, causing trouble. Although they do not take food, they nevertheless hunger and thirst and cause offences. These same spirits will rise up against the children of men and women because they have originated from them."

35

"From the days of slaughter, destruction and death of these giants, their spirits, having left the flesh, shall destroy without incurring judgement until the final day, the day of consummation – great judgement day of both the Watchers and the godless.

"Now, as to the Watchers who have sent you to intercede for them who were originally from heaven, say this to them: 'You have been to heaven but all the mysteries had not been revealed to you and those you knew are worthless, yet even these in the hardness of your hearts you have passed on to women and now because of them men and women work much evil on earth.' Say this also to them: 'You will have no peace!'"

36

Then I was taken to a place where there were beings like flaming fire. If they wished to they could change to appear like men. These brought me to the place of darkness and to a mountain with its tip reaching heaven. I saw then places of where there were light-giving bodies, a treasury of stars and thunder. In the very depths there was a fiery bow and arrows and their quivers; then a fiery sword and lightnings. From here I was taken to see the living waters and then to the fire of the west where the sun sets. Then I came to a river of fire flowing like water and discharging itself into the great sea in the west. From there I saw great rivers. One of these I came up to and to great darkness where no flesh exists. Slowly I saw mountains of darkness of the winter emerging and the source of the waters of the deep, flowing. From here was revealed the rivers of the earth and the mouth of the deep.

37

As I looked on I was shown the treasuries of all the winds, how God had provided the whole of creation and foundations of the earth with wind. There I saw the cornerstone of the earth; I saw the four winds that are said to bear the earth and whole atmosphere or firmament of the world. Like pillars of heaven they stretch across the world. I was shown the winds that are in space following the circumference of the sun and the stars. On the earth I watched the winds carrying the clouds; I even saw the paths of the angels. The next thing to be seen was a place which burns day and night – here there are seven mountains of magnificent stones: three toward the east, one of which was coloured, one pearl and one jacinth; those to the south were of red stone. But the middle one reached to heaven like the throne of God. It was made of alabaster and the summit was sapphire. I also saw a flaming fire.

38

Beyond these mountains there is a region near the area called the great earth; here the heavens are said to have been completed. There's a deep abyss with columns of heavenly fire. Among these I saw columns of fire fall, the size of which I couldn't even guess. Beyond here was another place, which did not seem to have anything above or below it, and definitely no sign of water or bird life – just a horrible waste land. As I looked on I saw seven stars like great burning mountains. I asked the angel who stood next to me what this was all about. The angel spoke to me: "This place is the end of heaven and earth: this has become a prison for the stars and the host of heaven. The stars you see rolling over the fire are they which have violated and gone beyond the bounds of the Lord's Commandments. They did not go forth at their appointed times. Therefore He was angry with them and has bound them until the great day of judgement and day of completion when all will be made perfect, even if it takes ten thousand years!"

Now Uriel stood next to me and said to me, "Here shall stand the angels who have attached themselves to women. For their spirits now assume many different forms for defiling mankind and shall lead many astray into sacrificing to demons pretending they are gods. They shall stand here ready for the great day of judgement. The judgement will make an end to them. As for the women they had, they who were led astray will become sirens [i.e., dangerously fascinating temptresses and irresistible women] to many."

I, Enoch, alone have seen this vision of the ends of all things. No man has seen what I have seen.

39

Now much have I seen but much have I also been told. What I shall share with you next is the names and functions of the Seven Archangels. These are the names of the Holy Angels who keep watch: Uriel, who watches over the world and that which is called Tartarus; Raphael, who is over the spirits of men; Raguel, one of the Holy Angels, who will take revenge on the world of the luminaries; Michael, he is set over the best part of mankind and over chaos [now a science and recognised as such by scientists]; Saraqael presides over those spirits who sin in the spirit; then there is Gabriel [known to the world through Scripture], he is over Paradise, the serpents and the Cherubim; lastly there is Remiel, said to be over they that rise [from the dead?].

40

I now went to a place where things were chaotic. I saw there something really horrible: there was neither anything above nor earth below, but a place chaotic and horrible. Here I saw seven stars bound together like great mountains burning with fire. I then asked the angel by my side, "What sin bound these together and why are they bound like this?"

Uriel, one of the holy angels who was with me and who was over me, answered me: "Why, Enoch, do you ask this question and why are you so eager for the truth?" There was a brief pause, then he continued, "These are the number of the stars who have transgressed against the Lord and will be bound for ten thousand years."

41

From here I was transported to another place, which was even more horrible than the last one. Here I saw a great fire blazing along a narrow opening up to the abyss. Here, as before, great columns of fire descended. I knew not its extent or magnitude. I spoke to the angel acting as my guide: "What a frightening place this is!"

The angel was Uriel and he answered, "Enoch, why are you so fearful of this place?"

I looked at him and at our surroundings. "Well, it fills me with fear and it seems to be a place full of pain!"

"You see, Enoch," he replied, "this is the prison of the angels and here they will be imprisoned for ever!"

We went on to yet another place in the west, another great high mountain of hard, solid rock. I saw in it four hollow places, deep and wide but very smooth to the touch. Three were dark inside but the fourth one was bright and inside it was a fountain of water.

I asked Uriel about these hollows: "How smooth these hollows feel to the touch; three of them are dark inside, why?" He did not answer, but Raphael came to me and answered me: "These hollow places have been created for this purpose. That the spirits of the souls of the dead should assemble in there, as will the souls of the children of men. They will dwell here until the great day of judgement comes upon them."

As I looked harder into the hollows I saw the spirits of the children of men who were dead but yet their voices were raised up toward heaven in pleading. One particular spirit of a dead man cried out to heaven and I asked who he was. Raphael looked at the man, then spoke to me in a quiet voice: "This is the spirit of Abel. Remember he was killed by his brother Cain? He is crying out for justice; he requests that the family tree of his brother be destroyed."

I looked further into the hollows and saw that each spirit was separated from the others and I asked why this was. Raphael answered me again, with much patience. He told me that the three hollows were made like that to separate the dead. The fourth and brighter hollow was made for the spirits of the righteous and a spring of water is there for them.

"Now, I will explain something to you, Enoch. When sinners die and are buried in the earth and judgement has not been executed on them in their earthly life span, here they are set apart in great pain till the great day of judgement and punishment. Those who are accused shall receive scourgings and torments, particularly those who curse, and there will be retribution for their spirits. The Lord will bind them forever. For those who were killed by men in their lifetime, they will make disclosures concerning their destruction. This is available for people who are not righteous but sinners. Of these, their spirits shall not be destroyed on the great day of judgement, but neither will they be raised but shall be bound forever."

I then blessed the Lord our God, saying, "I bless the Lord of Glory. Blessed be my Lord, the lord of righteousness who rules for ever!"

42

I went to a place in the west, where I saw a fire that never ceased. I saw another angel with me, whose name was Raguel. I said to him, "What is this fire for?" He answered me and said: "This fire that is before us is used upon the Luminaries of Heaven [persons having spiritual influence]."

43

From here I travelled to another place, where he showed me a mountain range of fire which burnt unceasingly. Beyond the fire I saw seven magnificent mountains, all different from one another. The stones of the mountains appeared magnificent and beautiful. Three mountains faced the east, one being based upon another. Three faced towards the south, one upon another. Deep, rough ravines went between these sets of mountains. The seventh mountain was set in the midst of these other mountains. It was far higher than any other mountain in the range and in a way resembled a throne in appearance. Around this mountain I saw a circle of fragrant-smelling trees. Amongst these trees was one particular type of tree that I could not recognise and it had a fragrance all of its own. I was told that its blooms, leaves and the very wood of the tree will never wither. As I looked it bore fruit similar to dates and they looked beautiful.

"This tree is so beautiful and fragrant and so delightful in appearance." Michael stood by my side and spoke to me. "Enoch, why do you say such about this tree and its fragranc, You wish to learn the truth?"

"I wish to know everything, especially about this tree."

"This high mountain which you see, whose very summit is like the throne of God, is His throne. The throne of the Holy Great One, the Lord of Glory and Eternal King. Here He will come to sit when He visits the earth with goodness. As for the beautiful fragrance of this tree, no mortal is permitted to touch it until the Great Day of Judgement. This day He will take vengeance on all, bring everything to its conclusion and accomplishment. Then it shall be given to the righteous and holy. To the elect He shall give its fruit to them to eat. The tree will be removed to the Temple of the Lord. Then they shall rejoice with all joy and gladness.

"They will then enter the Holy Place. The tree's fragrance shall be in their bones and they shall live a long life in earthly terms. In their days there shall be no longer any sorrow or plague, no torment or calamity shall touch them."

I was so filled with awe that I praised the Lord my God there and then, who had created all things and who will fulfil His promises.

44

From that wonderful tree I travelled on to the middle of the earth and saw a most blessed place where there were trees with branches in bloom. I also saw a dismembered tree close by. Here I saw what appeared to be a Holy Mountain. Underneath it and to the east was a stream flowing due south. As I looked toward the east I saw another mountain far higher than this one. Between them was a narrow ravine. Within the ravine ran another stream, which disappeared under the mountain.

I then turned to the west and there too was a mountain. It was smaller and lower than the others were. A deep, dry ravine separated the mountains and another ravine was at the very ends of the three mountains. As I studied these ravines, they appeared to be deep and narrow, having been formed of hard rock, and treeless. It all appeared so marvellous to me. I asked my companion what was the object of this place that was entirely filled with trees and the valley so dry and barren, that yet it seemed accursed.

Uriel stood next to me and he told me that this "accursed" valley is for those who are accursed forever. For they would all be assembled here who utter things against the Lord, such unseemly words and harsh words against Him and His Glory. For this will be their place of judgement. The Great Day of Judgement shall come upon them and the spectacle of righteous judgement shall be seen in the presence of the righteous for them to see forever. Here the godly will see judgement and glorify the Lord of Glory, the Eternal King. In these days of judgement the righteous will bless the Lord of Glory for His mercy in accordance with which He has assigned them their lot."

Again I was filled with great wonder at the majesty and awesomeness of our God and I cried out and blessed the Lord of Glory.

45

My journey took me now to the east into the midst of the mountain range within a desert. I saw a wilderness that appeared solitary and full of trees and plants. Water then appeared to be gushing down from above like a watercourse, which in turn flowed towards the north-west. There it caused clouds and dew to drop upon the land on all sides. I travelled onwards to a place in the desert, approaching it to the east of the mountain range. Here I came across trees exhaling the scent of frankincense and myrrh. These trees were very similar to almond trees. Travelling on, I went forward easterly and came to a valley full of water. Here I saw a tree the colour of mastic [the colour of resin, such as that produced by the mastic tree]; also on the sides of valleys I saw fragrant cinnamon. From here I continued to the east.

On the way I saw other mountains, amongst which were groves of trees from which flowed nectar, which is named Sarara and Galbanum. Beyond these mountains there was another upon which I saw aloe trees [the modern eagle wood of South-East Asia, producing a fragrant odour when burnt]. All the trees were full of stacte [sweet spice used in making incense]. When I burnt some of this, it smelt sweeter than any fragrance I have smelt before.

I then looked toward the north. I looked over a range of mountains to a range of seven mountains that were full of choice nard and fragrant trees with cinnamon and pepper.

46

I travelled on, going over the summits of all these mountains towards the east. I passed over the Erythraean Sea [the Persian Sea and Indian Ocean] and far from it. I even passed over the angel Zotiel. Eventually I came to a garden.

This garden was called the Garden of Righteousness and it was full of trees. Beyond these trees were two large trees – they were very great and beautiful, glorious to view, nay, magnificent! One tree was the Tree of Knowledge and whosoever did eat of this holy fruit would know great wisdom. This tree was as high as a fir and its leaves were like those of the carob tree. The fruit of this tree was like clusters of the vine, very beautiful and having a fragrance that penetrated near and far.

It was so wonderful here. I had to admit to my guide how wonderful it was to me. "How beautiful is this tree and so attractive!"

Raphael was by my side and he answered me: "This is the tree of wisdom, of which your father, old in years, and your mother aged, together ate of the fruit and the wisdom they received opened their eyes and for the first time they realised they were naked. For this forbidden act they were driven out of the garden."

47

I travelled to what appeared the ends of the earth, seeing there great beasts each being different from one another. So too were the birds of the air, so beautiful in form and sound. I looked towards the horizon, like the end of the earth where the heavens meet the earth. Then I saw the portals of heaven open and witnessed how the stars of heaven come forth and I counted the portals. Then I wrote down all their outlets, for each individual star. Each according to their numbers and their names, their courses and positions, their times and their months. All this I was shown and taught by the angel Uriel. He showed all things to me and he wrote them down for me. He wrote down their names for me, their laws and their companies.

48

From there I went and travelled towards the north until I came to a great and glorious device. For here were three portals of heaven open. Through each of them proceeded the north winds. They that blew were cold and filled with hail, frost, snow, dew and rain. Out of one portal the winds blew for good, but through the other two portals the winds blew with a vengeance and they will afflict the earth. They blew with violence.

To the west I saw three more portals of the heaven with the same number of outlets. Then to the south. Again three portals to the heavens and exactly the same as before. From these came dew, rain and wind. Finally to the east, and here three eastern portals open and small portals above. Through each of these small portals pass the stars of heaven who run their course following a path which has been shown to them.

For all that I had seen and witnessed I blessed the Lord of Glory and thanked Him for all His great and glorious wonders. I thanked the Lord for showing how great His works are to me and to His angels and to the spirits of men, that we may all praise and glorify our God. To praise Him for His creation that we who see His great works will praise and worship Him forever.

49

Now the time came for a second vision, the vision of wisdom, which I, Enoch, the son of Mahalalel, the son of Cainan, son of Enos, son of Seth and the son of Adam. These are the beginning of the words of wisdom, which I share with all who dwell upon the earth. Hear me men of old, men of the present time and of the future, the words of the Holy One, and witnessed by the Lord of Spirits. Never before has such wisdom been given by the Lord of Spirits as I have received according to my ability and insight, according to the good pleasure of the Lord of Spirits, by whom the lot of eternal life has been given to me.

50

Three parables have been given to me and these I impart to all who dwell on the earth. The First Parable is this. When the congregation of the righteous shall appear, sinners shall be judged for their sins and shall be driven from the face of the earth. When the Righteous One appears before the righteous whose works hang upon the Lord of Spirits, light shall appear to the righteous and the elect who dwell on the earth.

Where, then, will be the dwelling place for sinners and those who have denied the Lord? For it would have been good for them if they had never been born. The secrets of the righteous shall be revealed and sinners will be judged. The godless will be driven from the presence of the righteous and the elect. From that time those who possess the earth shall no longer be powerful, neither will they be exalted as they had been in the past. They will not be able to look at the Lord, as His Light will appear and shine on the righteous and the elect of God. From that time shall kings and all the mighty of the earth perish. They will be given into the hands of the righteous and the holy. Such sinners and ungodly people will not be able to seek mercy from the Lord of Spirits, for their life would be at an end.

In those days the elect and holy children will descend from the high heaven and their seed will become one with the children of men.

I, Enoch, received books of zeal and wrath, the books of disquiet and expulsion.

"Mercy shall not be given to them!" said the Lord of Spirits.

51

As if in a whirlwind, I was carried from the face of the earth and I found myself at the very end of heaven. Here another vision came to me.

I saw the dwelling places of the holy and resting places of the righteous. I also saw these dwellings with His righteous angels and their resting places with the holy. Here they petitioned, interceded and prayed for the children of men, and righteousness flowed before them like water. It is like this forever and ever.

In that place I saw the Elect One of righteousness and of faith. His dwelling place being under the wings of the Lord of Spirits. In all His days righteousness shall prevail. Standing before Him were countless numbers of righteous and the elect. They are before Him forever and they are strong and bright as fiery lights: they shall bless Him always. Their very lips extol the name of the Lord of Spirits. It was so wonderful, I wanted to dwell there also and I petitioned the Lord that this be granted to me. This has been established concerning me before the Lord of Spirits. I then praised the Lord enthusiastically as He has destined me for blessing and glory according to His good pleasure. Then for a long time my eyes took in that place and again I thanked and blessed the Lord my God and said to Him, "Blessed is He, and may He be blessed from the beginning and for evermore. There is no ceasing with the Lord. He knows before the world was created what is forever and what will be from generation to generation. Those who do not sleep bless the Lord. They who stand before your Glory, may they bless, praise and extol you evermore, saying: 'Holy, holy, holy is the Lord of Spirits: He fills the earth with spirits.'"

52

As I looked I saw many who never sleep; they stand before Him and bless Him and say: "Blessed be you and blessed be the name of the Lord, for ever and ever." I had to hide my face for the spectacle I could no longer bear.

Gradually I managed to look again and I saw thousands and thousands, a multitude beyond number standing before the Lord. Then on four sides of the Lord of Spirits I saw what I can only describe as four presences, each one being different. An angel who was with me made known to me their names and showed me all hidden things.

Then I heard the voices of these presences as they praised the Lord of Glory, like this. The first voice cried out, "Blessed is the Lord of Glory for ever and ever!" The second voice blessed the Elect One and the elect ones who hang upon the Lord of Spirits. The third voice prayed and interceded for those who dwell on the earth and made a humble petition of the Lord of Spirits. From the fourth I heard fending off the Satans and forbidding them to come before the Lord to accuse them who live on the earth.

I was a little perplexed at what I had seen and I asked the angel who was with me, "Who are these four presences which I have seen and whose words I have written down?"

The angel answered me: "This first is Michael, the merciful and long-suffering; the second, who is set over all the diseases and all the wounds of the children of men, is Raphael. The third, set over all the powers, is Gabriel and the fourth, who is set over repentance with the hope of those who inherit eternal life, is named Phanuel." These presences are therefore angels of the Lord of Spirits.

53

After this I saw all the secrets of the heavens, how the kingdom is divided and how the actions of mankind are weighed in the balance. Then I was shown the mansions of the elect and the mansions of the holy. As I looked closer I saw all sinners being driven from there, for they deny the name of the Lord. These are dragged away for punishment, which proceeds from the Lord God.

54
A short while later I saw the secrets of the lightning and of thunder, the winds and how they are divided to blow across the world along with clouds and dew. I saw them proceed and watched them saturate the dusty earth. Then I saw closed chambers out of which the winds are divided. A chamber of hail and winds, then the chamber of the mist and of the clouds that hover over the earth. Then I saw chambers for the sun and moon, how one is more superior to the other. The orbit, how this never changes and how they interact with one another as though bound by an oath. The sun is set in its place according to the commandment of the Lord. The orbit of the moon, its path giving us day and night. These appeared to give praise and thanks to our Lord.

For the sun can be either a blessing or a curse. Likewise the light of the moon can be light to the righteous or darkness to sinners according to the word of the Lord of Spirits, who made a separation between light and dark and the division of the spirits of mankind. He does give strength to the spirits of the righteous in the name of His Righteousness. Neither angel nor any power hinders Him, for He appoints a judge for them all and He judges them all before him. Thanks be to God!

55
It seemed strange that wisdom found no place where she might dwell; then a place was assigned to her in the heavens. Was this for my understanding?

She went forth to make her dwelling among the children of men but found no dwelling place. She returned to her place and sat among the angels.

Now I saw her, who is called Unrighteousness. She set forth from her chambers for no particular mortals but they whom she found, and she dwelled with them like rain in a desert and like dew on a thirsty land.

56

I saw lightnings and the stars of heaven and how He called them all by their names. How they were weighed in a righteous balance according to their proportions of light. I saw the width of their spaces and the day they were to appear and how their revolution produces lightning according to the number of the angels. Also how they react with one another. Then I asked the angel who was with me, "What are these?"

The angel replied: "The Lord of Spirits has shown you their parabolic meaning, for these are the names of the holy who dwell on the earth and believe in the name of the Lord for ever." Something else appeared strange to me, and that was how some stars arise and become lightnings and cannot return to their original form.

[The parable of the stars signifies the holy ones. Will they be as numerous as stars?]This is the end of the first parable.

57

The Second Parable concerns those who deny the name of the dwelling of the holy ones and the Lord of Spirits [Almighty God]. For they will not ascend into heaven, neither will they dwell on the earth. Such is the lot of sinners and those who have denied the name of the Lord. They are to be preserved for the day of suffering and tribulation.

On that day, My Elect One [Son of Man] shall sit on the throne of Glory. But sinners and the evil ones shall not set a foot on or near the throne. The Lord has provided and satisfied with peace His righteous ones and has caused them to dwell with Him. For sinners, there is judgement impending with the Lord and He will destroy them from the face of the earth.

58

Suddenly, I saw one who had a head of days. His head was white like pure wool and with Him was another whose face had the appearance of a man. His face was full of graciousness like one of the holy angels.

I asked the angel by my side about this Son of Man. Who was he and why the Head of Days? He turned and spoke to me: "This is the Son of Man who has righteousness, and who reveals all the treasures of that which is hidden because he is the chosen one of God. Whose lot has the pre-eminence before the Lord our God in righteousness forever. This Son of Man whom you have seen shall raise up the kings and the mighty from their seats, the strong from their thrones. He shall loosen the reins held by the strong and break the teeth of all sinners. He shall put down kings from their thrones and from their kingdoms, they who refuse to extol and praise Him [they without faith in Him]. They who do not humbly acknowledge Him, for He provided them with their kingdoms. He will put down the strong and fill them with shame, for darkness shall be their new dwelling place. They shall have their bed infected by worms so that they may not be able to rise up from the bed. All this because they refuse to acknowledge the Lord their God.

"These are they who will judge all people and spirits. Those who raise their hands against the Most High, whose deeds are unrighteous and who use their riches to acquire power. For their faith is in the gods whom they have made with their hands. In doing so, they deny Almighty God and they persecute the houses of His congregations. They afflict the faithful who live and have faith in the Lord our God."

59

In those days the prayers of the righteous and the blood of the righteous shall rise to the Lord of Spirits. All they who are holy, dwelling in the heavens, shall join together in one voice in supplication and prayer, praising and giving thanks to Almighty God, on the behalf of the righteous on earth. Their prayers shall not be in vain, for His judgement will be on their behalf and they shall not ever suffer.

60

Then I saw the Head of Days seated upon the throne of His Glory. Before Him were opened the books of the living. With Him stood the Host of heaven, His counsellors. Their hearts were filled with joy because of the number of the righteous and the hearing of their prayers together with their blood, which had been required by the Lord.

61

In this very place I saw the fountain of righteousness, which is inexhaustible. All around were other fountains, fountains of wisdom. Those who were thirsty drank of this water and they were filled with wisdom. From here, their dwelling place was to be with the righteous and holy and the elect of God. The hour had come when the Son of Man was to be named in the presence of Almighty God, the God of Spirits, His name before the Head of Days.

In fact, the Lord, even before the creation of the sun, stars and heaven, knew His name itself. For He shall become a staff to the righteous for them to lean on and trust for their support that they may not fall. He shall be the light of the Gentiles and hope to those who are troubled in heart and mind and a living hope to all. For all who dwell in the world shall fall down before Him and worship Him. They will praise and bless Him, singing songs to the Lord of Spirits.

62

For this reason has He been chosen and hidden from all creation for evermore. Yet God will reveal Him only to the righteous and the holy ones. For the Son of Man has preserved the lot of the righteous. For they have hated and despised this world of unrighteousness. They have hated its entire works and wicked ways in the name of Almighty God. For only in His name can they be saved and through His good pleasure regarding their life.

63

In those days to come, the countenance of rulers of the earth shall become downcast, for the strong shall possess the land through the works of their hands. Yet at the appointed day they shall experience anguish and affliction and they shall not be able to save themselves. For the Lord shall hand them over to His elect and as straw on a fire they shall burn before His face. Like lead in water, they shall sink before the faces of all righteous people. After this, there shall be peace on earth for they will have been removed from its sight, to sink and rise no more. All this because they denied the one true God, the Lord of Spirits and His Anointed One. The name of the Lord is blessed!

64

Wisdom shall be poured out like water and the glory of God shall never fail. For He is mighty in all things and in all secrets of righteousness.

All unrighteousness shall disappear like a shadow for ever, for the Elect One of God stands before the Lord of Spirits, His glory is for ever and ever and before all generations. For in Him dwells the spirit of wisdom, the spirit of insight, understanding and of might. The spirits of all the righteous who have fallen asleep are with Him. He shall judge all secret things for none can utter a lying word before Him, the Elect One of God.

65

When the time comes, the days of great change will take place for both the holy and the elect of God. All their days shall be full of light and glory and honour will come to the holy.

Then will come the day of affliction in which evil that has been bound up like treasure will visit sinners, but the righteous will be victorious in the name of the Lord. He will ensure all will witness this, that those seeing will come to repent of their sins and those things they have done which have wronged many in their lives. For such people will have no honour through the good name of the Lord yet through Him they could be saved. For those who repent of their sinfulness He will have compassion on them, and great is His compassion!

As for His judgement, He is righteous in all His judgements. Such judgement will fall on those who refuse to repent and they will all perish before Him. For He has said, "I will have no mercy on them!"

66

Also at that time, the earth will give back all that the Lord has entrusted to it – even that place where the dead dwell shall give back to the Lord what it has received. Also from the depths of Hell all shall be given back to the Lord. When this takes place, the Elect One shall rise and He will choose the righteous and the holy from among them. For this will be the day when they will be saved.

The Elect One shall sit upon the throne of Almighty God and from His mouth shall come all secrets of wisdom and counsel, for the Lord of Spirits has given them to Him and glorified Him.

67

Great and wondrous things shall happen in the world, for the very mountains will appear to leap like rams and hills will seem as though they are skipping like lambs satisfied with milk. The faces of all angels in heaven shall shine with joy. The very earth will rejoice and the righteous will then dwell on the earth and with them the Elect of God will walk alongside them.

68

Now these days passed, in the place where I had seen all the visions – for I had been carried off in a whirlwind towards the west. Then my eyes saw all the secret things of heaven that will then happen: a mountain of iron, one of silver, gold, soft metal and lead.

I asked the angel who was standing by my side what these things were, what they meant. He answered me and said: "All these things which you have seen will serve the dominion of His Anointed One, that He may be potent and mighty on the earth." Then he looked at me and said, "Wait a little while and you will see before you many secret things which surround the Lord of Spirits. For these mountains which you see shall, including the mountain of copper, be in the presence of the Elect One. Like wax before a fire, like water which streams down from above the mountains, all shall become powerless at His feet. For none shall be saved in those days. No one saved by either their gold, or by silver, none will escape. There shall be no iron for war, no armour. Bronze shall not be serviceable. Tin will cease to be of any service to mankind and lead will cease to be desired. For in those days to come they will be destroyed from the surface of the earth. All this when the Elect One appears before the face of the Lord of Spirits."

69

I then saw a deep valley with an opening like mouths. All who dwell on the earth and sea, upon islands, shall bring to Him gifts and presents, tokens of homage, yet that deep valley shall never be filled.

However, they commit lawless deeds, and the sinners will oppress them until they are destroyed before the face of God. For they shall be banished from the face of the earth. Their perishing will go on forever and ever.

I saw there all the angels of punishment and they prepared instruments of Satan. I was concerned by what I saw. So I asked the angel who was with me about this. I said to him, "Who are they preparing these instruments for?"

He answered, "They prepare these for the kings and all the mighty of this earth for their destruction! After this the Righteous and Elect One shall cause the house of His congregation to appear, for they will no longer be hindered in the name of the Lord, by these kings and mighty ones of the earth."

70

Then I gradually turned to look at another part of the earth. There I saw a deep valley with burning fire. To this place they brought these kings and the mighty and began to cast them into this deep valley. I was then shown how the instruments were made. Iron chains of immeasurable weight. I turned to my angel guide and said, "Who are these chains made for?"

"These are being prepared for the hosts of Azazel. They will take them and cast them into the abyss of complete condemnation. They shall cover their jaws with rough stones as commanded by the Lord of Spirits. On that great day, Michael, Gabriel, Raphael and Phanuel shall take hold of them and cast them into the burning furnace. For the Lord will take vengeance on them for their unrighteousness as subjects of Satan and for leading many astray who dwelt on the earth."

71

In those days shall punishment come from the Lord of Spirits, for He will open all the chambers of waters, which are above the heavens, and the fountains beneath the earth. Now the waters above the heavens are masculine; the waters beneath the earth feminine. The waters were to destroy all who lived on the earth, and they were to recognise their unrighteousness. However, the Head of Days repented and said, "In vain had I destroyed all who dwell on the earth. From now on I will not destroy them but have set a sign in the sky. This shall be a pledge of good faith between me and all people so long as heaven remains above the earth. This shall be in accordance with my Command."

Then I saw hosts of angels of punishment who held scourges and chains of iron and bronze. I asked a question of the angel who was with me. "To whom are these who hold the scourges going?"

I was surprised when the angel gave me this reply: "To their elect and beloved ones that they may be cast into the chasm of the abyss of the valley. Then the valley will be filled with the elect and beloved for the days of their lives will then be at an end. The days of their leading astray will not be reckoned. For in those days to come, angels will return and hurl themselves to the east upon them that set themselves up against Israel. They will stir up in their leaders a spirit of unrest who shall break forth as lions from their lairs and as hungry wolves among flocks. They shall tread underfoot the land [Israel] of the elect ones. They shall use this land like a threshing-floor and a highway. Yet the city of His righteousness shall be a hindrance to them and they shall fight amongst themselves. Their right hand shall be strong against themselves. For a man shall not know his brother, nor a son his father or mother. There will be many of their dead. All their punishment will not be in vain. In those days the underworld of the dead [Sheol] shall open its jaws and they will all be swallowed up. Their destruction shall be at an end. In the presence of the elect ones, the underworld will devour the sinners before their sight."

72

Then I saw a number of wagons with men riding in them travelling on the winds of the east, from the west to the south. The noise of these wagons was great and all heard them. When the turmoil took place the holy ones from heaven remarked on it. Then the pillars of the earth were moved from their place; the sound of this was heard from one end of heaven to the other. All this took place within one day! All fell down and worshipped the Lord of Spirits, God Almighty.

This is the end of the Second Parable.

73

Now I come to the Third Parable. I found myself speaking the Third Parable concerning the righteous and the elect. For blessed are you who are the righteous and the elect of God, for glorious shall be your lot. For the righteous will be in the light of the sun and the elect, in the light of eternal life. The days of their life shall be unending and the days of the holy without number. They shall seek the light and find righteousness with the Lord. The righteous shall have peace in the name of the Eternal Lord.

After this it will be said to the holy of heaven that they should seek out the secrets of righteousness, which is the heritage of faith, for it has become as bright as the sun that shines upon the earth. For all darkness is past and there shall be a light that never ends. There will be no limit to the days of their life. All darkness will be destroyed, for the light has been established by the Lord of Spirits, for it is the light of uprightness, established now for ever before the Lord.

74

In those days my eyes saw the secrets of the lightnings and of the light; also the judgements that are executed. Be it light for a blessing or a curse according to the Will of God. Here I also saw the secrets of thunder, how it resounds above in heaven. He showed me the judgements executed on the earth. Some for well-being and blessing, some for a curse according to the Word of the Lord. I was shown then the secrets of lights and lightnings, for they lighten for blessing and for satisfying.

75

[This next section is believed to be a fragment of the Book of Noah, which I have decided to include in this book for the reader's interest.]

It was the year 500, in the seventh month, on the fourteenth day of the month in the life of Enoch. In a vision I saw how a mighty quaking made the heaven of heavens to quake, and the Most High, the angels – a thousand thousands and ten thousand times ten thousand – were anxious and there was a lot of unrest. The Head of Days sat upon His throne of Glory and all the angels and the righteous stood around Him. As I looked, I started to tremble violently and I was full of fear, to such an extent that I collapsed to the ground face down. At this point Michael sent an angel to raise me up and I came to. You see, I was not able to endure all this I was seeing.

Once on my feet again, Michael came to speak to me: "Why are you unable to cope with this vision? For until this day lasted the day of His mercy, for He has been merciful and long-suffering towards those who live on the earth. For when the day, power and punishment and the judgement come, for which the Lord has prepared for those who do not accept His Laws but deny righteous judgement, for those who take His name in vain – that day is prepared for the elect ones a covenant, but for sinners an inquisition! At that appointed time, the Lord of Spirits' punishment shall rest upon them. It will not come in vain for it shall slay children with their mothers and the children with their fathers. After this the judgement shall take place according to His mercy and His patience."

76

Then were two monsters parted, a female named Leviathan, caused to dwell in the abysses of the oceans and over the fountains of the waters. The male is called Behemoth, who occupies a waste of wilderness named Duidain [known as the Land of Nod, to the east of Eden]. Here, on the east of the garden, where the elect and righteous dwell, is where my grandfather was taken up, the seventh from Adam.

I then begged the other angel to show me the might of these monsters and how they parted on one day and one being cast into the abysses of the sea and the other onto dry land. He turned and spoke to me and said he understood my desire to know what is hidden. Then an angel showed me what was hidden, what is first and last in heaven, in the height and then beneath the earth in the depths. To the ends and foundation of the heavens. The chambers of the winds, how they are divided and weighed. The way the portals of the winds are reckoned, each according to the power of the wind, and the power of the lights of the moon and according to the power that is fitting and the divisions of the stars according to their names, and how all the divisions are divided. And the thunders, according to the places where they fall, and the divisions of the lightnings, their host, that they must obey at once. Thunder has an assigned place to rest while waiting for its peal. Thunder and lightning are inseparable, and although not one and undivided, they both go together through the spirit and separate not. For when the lightning lightens, thunder utters its voice and the spirit enforces a pause during the peal, dividing equally between them, for its treasury is like the sand and each one of them as it peals is bridled and controlled by the spirit towards the many areas of the earth.

It must be realised that the spirit of the sea is masculine and strong, according to the might of his strength. Like a rein, it is drawn back one moment then driven forward and dispersed.

Now concerning other elements. The spirit of the hoarfrost is an angel and the angel of hail is good. Snow has a spirit who leaves its chamber on account of its strength. For here is a special spirit within that descends from it like smoke; we call it frost. Yet mist is not part of these spirits but apart. Its course is oppressive both in light and in darkness, in winter and summer. At the ends of heaven the spirit of dew has its dwelling and has a connection with the spirit of rain. Its course is in all seasons of the earth. Clouds of mist and rain, one gives to the other. When the spirit of rain goes forth from its chamber, the angels come and open the chamber to lead it out. Once it has run its course, it unites with the water on the earth. The waters on the earth are there for all that dwells on the earth, for nourishment for the earth, and come from the Most High, who is in heaven. There is a set measure for the rain and the angels are responsible for it.

All these things were shown to me in the Garden of the Righteous. With me was the angel of peace, who spoke to me: "These two monsters are prepared to conform to the greatness of God, and they shall feed." [End of the Book of Noah fragment.]

77

Now I saw long cords had been given to certain angels and they took wings and flew, travelling north. I was puzzled and asked the angel who stood by my side, "Why have those angels taken these cords and gone off?"

The angel answered me: "They have gone to measure! They will return with the measures of the righteous, with the ropes of righteous to be given to the righteous. By these, the righteous will bind themselves to the name of the Lord of Spirits forever. The elect shall begin to dwell with the elect. The measures shall be given to faith, which strengthens righteousness. These measures shall reveal the secrets of the depths of the earth and those who have been destroyed by the desert and devoured by wild beasts and by the fish of the seas, that they may return and stay here for the day of the Elect One. For none shall be destroyed before the Lord of Spirits, for none can be destroyed."

78

Then all who dwell above in the heavens received a command, power, and one voice and one light like fire. Then with one voice they blessed, and praised and sang to the Lord with great enthusiasm and with wisdom. They were wise in what they said and in how they praised and glorified God. They were also wise in the spirit of life.

Then the Lord placed the Elect One on the throne of glory, for he is to judge all the works of the holy in heaven and he shall hold in balance their deeds, by which they are weighed. He shall lift up his countenance. He shall judge their secret ways according to the word of God, and their path according to the way of righteous judgement of the Lord of Spirits.

Then he shall summon all the host of heaven, all the holy ones above and the host of God. The Cherubim, Seraphim and Ophanin.

All the angels of power. The angels of principalities and kingdoms. Then the Elect One, and other powers on the earth and over water. On that great day shall rise one voice, to bless and glorify and be exalted in the spirit of faith, patience, wisdom and mercy. Also, in the spirit of judgement and of peace and goodness. All shall say, as of one voice, "Blessed is He, and may the name of the Lord of Spirits be blessed for ever and ever!"

Then they who sleep, but not being in heaven, shall bless Him. All the holy ones in heaven shall bless him. All the elect who shall dwell in the garden of life will bless Him. For great is the mercy of the Lord of Spirits. He is long-suffering. All His works and all that He has created He has revealed to the righteous and the elect. All in His Name, the Lord of Spirits.

79

Then the Lord commanded the kings, the mighty and the exalted and those who dwell on the earth and said this to them, "Open your eyes and lift up your horns and recognise the Elect One!"

The Lord seated him on the throne of His glory and the spirit of righteousness was poured out on him. The word of his mouth slays all sinners and all the unrighteous are destroyed from before his face. In that day all the kings and the mighty and all the exalted and those who hold power on the earth shall see and recognise him as he sits on the throne of His glory. He judges righteousness and no one will speak a lying word before Him.

Then pain will come to them, which is similar to a woman giving birth. Many will look at each other for they will be terrified and downcast for then the pain will grasp them. All this as they see the Son of Man sitting on His throne of glory. Now all kings and rulers and the mighty who dwell on the earth shall start to bless and worship Him, for previously He had been hidden to mankind. Then the Lord God preserved Him in the presence of His might and He shall be revealed to all the elect. All the elect and holy will be sown like a seed. The elect shall stand before Him on that day.

The kings and the mighty ones of the earth shall fall down before Him onto their faces, for they will worship and Him for his mercy.

Nevertheless, the Lord of Spirits will press hard upon them and they will hastily leave His presence for they will be filled with shame. There will be darkness across their faces. Then they will be delivered into the hands of the angels for punishment. Vengeance will be executed because they have oppressed His children and His elect. They will become a spectacle for the righteous and His elect, who will rejoice over them. They would have witnessed the wrath of the Lord; His sword is drunk with their blood. On that day the righteous and the elect will be saved and they shall never again see the face of a sinner or any unrighteous person.

The Lord of Spirits shall look after them and they will then dine and eat with the Son of Man. They shall lie down and rise up for ever and ever. They will have risen from the earth and no longer will they know distress or unhappiness. Their clothing will be a garment of glory and life, given them by the Lord God. Their garments will remain forever and never wear out, nor their glory fade.

80

Now those who were kings and the mighty on earth shall implore Him to grant them a little respite from the angels of punishment, so that they may fall down and worship Him. Also, a chance to confess their sins. He shall have mercy upon them and they will be given the opportunity to bless and glorify Him.

This is what they shall say: "Blessed is the Lord of Spirits and the Lord of Kings, the Lord of the mighty, Lord of the rich. The Lord of glory and wisdom, splendid in every secret thing is your power from generation to generation, forever and ever. Deep are all your innumerable secrets; your righteousness is beyond reckoning.

81

"We have now learnt that we should glorify and bless the Lord of kings and He who is king over all kings."

They shall continue by saying: "If only we had rest in order to glorify you and to give you thanks, to confess our faith before your glory! Now we long for a little rest but cannot find it. Even light has vanished from around us and we are dwelling in darkness, seemingly for ever and ever.

"It has been our own fault, we have not believed in Him, nor have we glorified the name of the Lord. All our hope has been in the sceptres of our kingdoms and in our own glory. In these times that we find ourselves in we suffer great tribulation, but He has not saved us and we find no opportunity for true confession.

"We know now that our Lord is true in all His works and in all His judgements and justice. His judgement is pure and true, as it has no respect of persons or their positions in the world. Now we pass away from before His face because of our ways and the ways we lived our lives. All our sins are reckoned up in His righteousness."

Then they will say to themselves: "Our souls are full of unrighteous gains, but it does not prevent us from descending from here to the place of the dead and its burdens."

Then their faces will become darkened and all will see their shame, even before the face of the Son of Man. They will all be driven from His presence and His sword shall drive them away. The Lord will then speak: "This is the ordinance and judgement with respect to the mighty and the kings and the exalted and those who possess the earth before the Lord of Spirits."

82

After this I heard an angel say, "These are the angels who descended to the earth who revealed what was hidden from the children of men. They seduced the children of men into committing sin."

I saw other forms whilst in this strange place.

83

[In this section, Enoch states how Noah was warned of the coming deluge and as to his own preservation.] In those days Noah saw the earth that it had sunk low and that its destruction was nigh. He got up and went to the end of the land and cried aloud to his grandfather Enoch. Three times Noah cried out, "Hear me, hear me, hear me!"

Then Noah cried out again to Enoch: "Tell me what it is that is going wrong on the earth, that the earth finds itself in such an evil condition."

There was a great commotion on the earth and a voice was heard coming from heaven. Noah fell to his face. There, standing beside him was his grandfather Enoch. He said to Noah, "Why have you cried out to me with such bitterness and crying?"

A command had gone out from the presence of the Lord concerning those who dwell on the earth, that their ruin be accomplished because they have learnt all the secrets of the angels, all the violence of the Satans, all their powers – the most secret ones – the secrets of the power of those who practise sorcery, witchcraft and those who make molten images for the whole earth. They were taught the secrets of how silver and soft metals were made and originated in the earth. Lead and tin are not produced from the earth, for it is a fountain that produces them and a pre-eminent angel stands in the fountain."

Now Enoch took hold of Noah by the hand and raised him up and said to him, "Go, for I have asked the Lord concerning this situation on the earth. He told me: 'Because of their unrighteousness, their judgement has been determined and will not be withheld from me. Because of the sorceries which they have been taught and learnt, the earth and those who dwell on it shall be destroyed.' These shall have no opportunity for repentance for what they have taught the people and are therefore damned. As for you, Noah, my son, the Lord of Spirits knows that you are pure and guiltless of such charges. You are destined to be counted as one of the holy. You will be preserved from those who dwell on the earth, and from your seed there will be kingships and great honours. There will come from your line a fountain of righteousness and the number of those who will be holy will be countless – for ever."

After this Noah was shown the angels of punishment who were prepared to come and let loose all the powers of water and the destruction of the earth and of all the evil ones who dwell on the earth. Then the Lord gave the command to these angels to control the waters and not allow them to rise.

Noah then departed from Enoch.

84

Then the word of God came to Noah: "Noah, I am aware of your life on earth, a life lived without blame, a life of love and uprightness. Now at this time, angels are making a wooden building and when it is completed I will place My hand on it and I shall preserve it. From this building shall come the seed of life and a change will come over the earth as it will not remain without inhabitants. I will bless your seed for ever and ever and I will spread abroad all those who will live with you. They will not be unfruitful on the face of the earth. They shall be blessed and they will multiply in My name."

Noah understood that the Lord would imprison those angels who had shown unrighteousness, in that burning valley which his grandfather Enoch had shown him, in the west, among the mountains of gold, silver, iron, soft metal and tin. Then Noah saw in that valley a great disturbance of water. When this was taking place, from that fiery molten metal and from the great disturbances in that place, there came a smell of sulphur from the waters. Through the valleys came streams of fire from where these fallen angels were placed.

Now these waters which smelled of sulphur shall serve the kings and the mighty and the exalted and all others dwelling on the earth. They were to be used for the healing of the body. [This place is believed to be Kallirrhoe, east of the Dead Sea, once the resort of Herod the Great.] Then it will be used as punishment for the spirit in later days and of the body. At the present time their spirits are filled with lust. When the time comes for their punishment, because they refused to believe in the name of the Lord, their bodies will become burnt [by hot sulphuric water] daily and increase in severity and their spirit will change correspondingly forever. This judgement comes because they believe in the pleasures of their bodies through lust, and in so doing they deny the Spirit of God.

Now these waters shall undergo a change. For whilst these fallen angels are punished within these waters, the temperature of the water will change and become suddenly cool.

Suddenly Noah heard the voice of Michael. The angel told him, "This judgement upon the fallen angels is a testimony for the kings and all the mighty who possess the earth. You see, these waters, which are being used as judgement, which have healed the body of kings and the causes of their lusts, will change and become a fire to burn forever. Those who use these waters will not believe nor accept that such a change could occur."

85

Now Enoch gave to Noah the secrets from the book and from the Parables that he had received. He put all this together in the Book of the Parables.

86

Now Raphael was speaking to Michael, and said, "The power of the spirit transports and makes me tremble because of the severity of the judgement of the secrets and of the angels [i.e., fallen angels, known as the Satans]. Who can endure such severe judgement which has been executed?"

Michael replied to this question from Raphael, "Who is he whose heart is not softened concerning this and not troubled by the word of judgement, particularly of those who led them out?"

They both came into the presence of the Lord and Michael spoke to Raphael: "I will not take their part in this, in front of our Lord. For the Lord of Spirits has been very angry with them because they acted as though they themselves were the Lord. For all that, that which was hidden has come to them for ever and ever. For no angel or man shall share in their portion, for they alone have received their judgement for ever and ever."

87

Now the names of the fallen angels were again given and the wrongs they had committed were known to all. What was mentioned was one particular fallen angel or Satan named Penemue. He had instructed mankind in writing with ink and paper. From then on many sinned from then until this very day. Why was it a sin? Men were not created for such a purpose, to give written confirmation of their good faith with pen and ink. We were created, so it appears, to be exactly like angels. To live a pure and righteous life and be free from death.

Through this knowledge we now perish and through this power we are consumed.

Another named angel, or Satan, was Kasdeja. He showed the children of men all the wicked ways of how to destroy spirits and how to affect the embryo in a woman's womb. Now another fallen angel mentioned was Kasbeel, a chief of the Oath called Biqa. This angel, whilst in heaven, asked Michael to show him the hidden name that he may proclaim it in the Oath. The idea being that once the name was revealed all would cause terror to those who hear or see it. Now he planned that the children of men became aware of it and of its power. The name of the Oath became Akae, and it was placed in the hands of Michael. These, now, are the secrets of the Oath.

They are strong through this Oath. And heaven was suspended before the world was created and forever. Through it the world was founded upon water. From the secret recesses of the mountains come beautiful waters, from the creation of the world and unto eternity.

Through this Oath the sea was created and for its foundation He set sand against the time of its anger so that it dares not pass beyond it from the creation of the world to eternity. Through this Oath are the depths made fast, so that they remain and move not from their place from eternity to eternity.

Through this Oath the sun and moon complete their course and do not deviate from their ordinance, from eternity to eternity. And through this Oath the stars complete their course, and He calls them by their names. They do answer Him from eternity to eternity.

In like manner the spirits of the water, the winds and all breezes, their paths from all quarters of the winds, the sounds of thunder and the light of lightnings, are all preserved. So are the chambers of hail, hoarfrost, mist, rain and dew. All believe and give thanks to the Lord of Spirits and they glorify Him for ever and ever.

This Oath is mighty over all things and through it all is preserved and their paths and their course are not destroyed

88

Now there was great joy amongst them and they blessed and glorified the name of the Son of Man, for He had been revealed to them all. He sat on the throne of His glory, and judgement was given to him. He caused sinners to pass away and He destroyed them from the face of the earth, and also those who had led the world astray.

They will be bound with chains and in their place for destruction. There they shall be imprisoned and all their deeds shall cease to exist on the earth. Then the earth will be free from all corruption.

For this reason the Son of Man will appear seated on the throne of Glory. All evil will pass away before His face and His word will go forth and He shall be strong before the Lord of Spirits, Almighty God.

Here ends the Third Parable of Enoch.

Now during His lifetime on earth, the name of the Son of Man was raised high in heaven. He was raised high on the chariots of the Spirit and from the earth His name vanished from amongst them. From that day I was no longer with them, but He set me between the two winds of the north and the west. Here angels took the cords to measure for me the place for the elect and righteous. There I saw the first fathers and the righteous ones who from the beginning dwelt in that place.

89

The time came again for my spirit to be lifted to the heavens, and there I saw the holy sons of God. They were stepping on fire and their clothing and faces were as white as snow.

Here I saw two streams of fire, and the light of that fire shone like hyacinth [orange variety of zircon]. So taken by this, I fell to my face before the Lord. Then Michael, an angel of the Lord, took me by the right hand and helped me rise, and he took me to see the secrets, the secrets of righteousness. He showed me all the secrets of the ends of heaven, all the chambers of the stars, luminaries and where they go before the face of the holy ones.

I found myself in the heaven of heavens and there before me was a structure built of crystals. Between these were tongues of living fire. I saw a sort of girdle that went round this structure, this house of fire. On all four sides were streams of fire.

As I looked, I could Seraphim, Cherubim and Ophannin. They never slept but guarded the throne of His glory. There were other angels – too many to be counted – all encircling that house.

I also saw Michael, Raphael, Gabriel and Phanuel – the holy angels who live above the heavens – come and go within that house. So did a number of other angels. With them I saw him who is the Head of Days, his head white and pure as wool, and wearing clothing which is indescribable.

Again I fell to my face on seeing him. I felt my whole body become relaxed and my spirit was transfigured. At this point I cried out loudly as I was filled by the Spirit and I blessed, glorified and gave praise. What I said was pleasing to the Lord. He then came forward with Michael, Gabriel, Raphael and Phanuel, along with a countless host of angels.

I saw another with the Lord and I called to an angel as he passed, and he came to me. I asked who it was that was with the Lord, and this is what he replied: "This is the Son of Man, who is born unto righteousness and righteousness abides over Him. The righteousness of the Lord shall never forsake Him. He proclaims peace in the name of the world to come, and peace comes in the name of the Most High, the Lord, since the creation of the world, for ever and ever. For He shall walk in the way of the Lord. All who believe in Him shall their dwelling be with Him and in Him is their heritage. They will never be separated from him but shall dwell with Him for ever and ever. All the righteous shall have peace and live an incorruptible life in the name of the Lord our God, for ever and ever."

90

[In the following details of the sun and moon, the writer believed in 364 days in a year.]

The book of the courses of the luminaries, their relationships to one another, each according to their class, dominion and the seasons, again according to their names and places of origin and according to their months, Uriel, the holy angel, who was with me, their guide, showed me all the laws from creation to eternity.

This is the first law. It concerns the sun, which rises from the eastern portal of heaven and sets at the western portal of heaven. I saw six portals in which the sun rises and six at its setting. The moon also rises and sets from these same portals. So do the leaders of the stars, all following each other accurately in corresponding order. To the right and left of these portals are windows.

To start with you have the sun, whose circumference is like that of the heaven. The sun is filled with illuminating and heating fire. There is a wind that drives the sun and assists its return through the north in order to reach the east. In this way it rises in the first month in the great fourth portal [sixth in the east]. In that fourth portal are twelve window openings, from which come a flame when they open in their season. So when the sun rises in the heaven it comes through the fourth portal thirty mornings in succession, setting likewise in the fourth portal of the west, of heaven.

During this period the day becomes longer and the night grows shorter. On that day that the daylight is longer than the night, by a ninth. The day amounts to exactly ten parts to the night's eight parts. Then the sun rises from the fourth portal and then sets in the fourth and returns to the fifth portal of the east for thirty mornings, then rises from it and sets in the fifth. The day then becomes longer by two parts to eleven parts and the night becomes shorter and amounts to seven parts. It returns to the east, entering the sixth portal. It then rises and sets in the sixth portal for thirty mornings. On that day the day becomes double the night, which is twelve parts to the night's six parts.

The sun rises to make the day shorter and then the night becomes longer. The sun rises and sets from the sixth portal for thirty mornings. When this is accomplished the day decreases by exactly one part, becoming eleven parts to the night's seven. The sun rises from the sixth portal in the west and travels to the east and rises in the fifth portal for thirty mornings and then sets in the west again in the fifth western portal. On that day the day decreases by two parts and becomes ten parts to the night's eight parts.

Now the sun rises from the fifth portal of the east and sets in the fifth portal of the west, and then rises in the fourth portal for one-and-thirty days, setting in the west. On this day the day is equal with the night in length. Therefore, day is nine parts and the night is also nine parts.

From this point in time the sun will rise from that same portal and set in the west and then makes a return journey to the east and will rise for thirty mornings from the third portal and set in the third portal of the west. Now the night will become longer than the day by ten parts, the day being eight parts long.

From the third portal in the east, the sun will rise and set, then return to the east to rise once again. Then the sun shall rise from the second portal of the east and set in the second portal of the west for thirty days. On that day the night amounts to eleven parts to the day's seven. Then on that day the sun rises from the third portal of the east and sets in the west. When it returns to the east it rises in the first portal of the east to the first portal of the west, where it sets. This will continue for thirty mornings. This results in the night being double of that of the day, that is, twelve parts night to six parts day. After this the sun is said to have completed its orbit in order to recommence this cycle.

This is the law and the course of the sun, all according to the command of the Lord.

91

After all this I saw another law dealing with the moon. The moon is driven by a wind and light is given in measures. The rising and the setting of the moon changes every month and, like the sun, when the moon's light is full [a full moon] it amounts to a seventh part of the light of the sun.

The first phase of the moon is in the east on the thirtieth morning from the same portal as the sun. One half of the moon travels by the seventh part and the rest of the moon is dark and without light. The moon keeps up with the sun, receiving half of one part of light that is called a lunar day. Then the moon sets with the sun and becomes invisible that night, with fourteen parts and the half of one part of light. On that day the moon will rise with exactly seven parts of light and in the remaining days becomes bright in the remaining thirteen parts.

92

All these things the angel Uriel showed me, and I wrote it all down. Now I shall explain to you the lunar year as told to me by the angel.

In single seventh parts the moon accomplishes giving light in the east and in single seventh parts darkness in the west. In certain months there are alterations to the sun's and moon's settings and in other months the moon follows a different path. For example, in two months the moon sets with the sun in the two middle portals and the third and the fourth. This continues for seven days and the moon then returns for a further seven days in light. The moon recedes from the sun and in eight days enters the sixth portal from which the sun rises.

Now, when the sun rises from the fourth portal the moon shows her light for seven days. This continues until the moon leaves the fifth portal and turns back in seven days to the fourth portal, and all is accomplished. In eight days' time the moon enters the first portal, returning again to the fourth in eight days' time.

If five years are added together the sun has an overplus of thirty days. All the days it has accrued in those five years, when they are full, amount to 364 days. Now, the overplus of the sun and of the stars amounts to six days. That is, in five years six days every year comes to thirty days. The moon falls behind the sun and stars to the number of thirty days.

The sun and stars work in with all the years exactly. They neither advance nor delay their order by a single day. In three years there are 1092 days; in five years, 1820 days; in eight years 2912 days. For the moon itself, three years amount to 1062 days, and in five years it is fifty days behind [i.e., to the sum of 1770 there is added (1000 and) sixty-two days]. In five years there are 1770 days, so that for the moon, the days in eight years amount to 2832 days [in eight years the moon falls behind by eighty-two days]. Therefore the year is always accurate and conforms exactly to a set plan and sets of thirty days.

93

There are leaders of the heads of the thousands, who are placed over all creation and the stars and planets [not believed to be angels]. They are also responsible for the four intercalary days [to resynchronise] which are not reckoned in a year. Owing to these days, mankind goes wrong in the calculation of the year. These luminaries are responsible for the exactness of the year that it is accomplished by the set 364 stations of the year. The signs, the times and the years and the days the angel Uriel had shown to me. Uriel also showed me the twelve openings of the sun whereby warmth covers the earth. Each one is delivering warmth and heat by opening at the correct time of the season.

There were many things shown to me, many I have spoken of earlier and now I will continue. Now the angel turned and spoke to me: "And now, my son, I have shown you everything and the law of all the stars of the heaven is completed."

He had shown me all the laws and revealed everything to me.

94

This I share with you – it concerns the perversion of nature and the heavenly bodies owing to the sin of mankind. When that great day of reckoning occurs, this shall take place.

In the days of sinners the year shall be shortened and the seed used on their land shall become tardy and all things on the earth shall alter and shall not appear in their correct time or season. Rain will be kept back from the earth and the fruits of the earth will be backward, for they will not grow in the correct season.

The moon, for once, will alter her course and not appear at the appointed time. The sun will only be seen in the west, at evening time, but will shine brighter than it has done before. Even the stars themselves will behave differently. All those on earth who are sinners will not notice such changes in the stars, while others will see and be troubled in their thoughts and they shall be changed in all their ways. Those who are troubled will see them as gods. Evil will come their way and so will punishment so destruction will come on them.

95

The angel spoke to me and said, "Observe, Enoch; see these heavenly words; read them and remember every individual fact."

I looked at these writings and read everything that was written and in front of me. I understood everything. I read the book of all the deeds of mankind and of the children of flesh. All they who dwell in the world and in every generation. It was so marvellous that I praised the Lord, the King of Glory forever, for He made the works of the world. I thanked Him and praised Him because of His patience and because of the children of men. After this I said, "Blessed is the man who dies in righteousness and goodness, concerning whom there is no book of unrighteousness been written, and against whom no day of judgement shall be found."

Then I was brought by seven holy ones who placed me on the earth before the door of my home. They said to me: "Declare everything to your son Methuselah and tell your children that no flesh is righteous in the sight of the Lord, for He is their Creator. You have one year to be with your son, until you give him your last command. Teach your children and record it for them and testify to them. Then in the second year they will come and take you away from them. Let your heart be strong, for the good shall announce righteousness to the good. All the righteous shall rejoice and congratulate one another. As for sinners, they shall die. Those who have no faith or deny it shall also go. However, those who practise righteousness shall die at the hands of sinners and on account of the deeds of godless men."

They departed from me and I came to speak to my people, blessing the name of the Lord.

96

I came to my son, Methuselah, and told him all that I had been shown. To help him remember I wrote books concerning all that had happened and all the things I told him. Then I told Methuselah that these books must be kept safely and made available to all the generations of the world.

Then I had imparted to him wisdom and to his children and their children to come. Such is this wisdom, that all who read it shall not sleep in ignorance but they may devour its wisdom as they do good food. Only this wisdom is better than any fine food, for it is food for the spirit that will last.

97

For blessed are all the righteous and they who walk in the way of righteousness and not in the ways of sin and sinners. For all their days are reckoned. For sinners will lead men into falsehood but men will not recognise their actions and deeds as such, for every year of a sinner's life is recorded forever. The account of their lives is accurate, as are the orbits of sun, moon and stars, for He has power over them all.

98

Over all the luminaries are four leaders who are responsible for leading them throughout seasons and festivals of the year. These leaders are responsible for one part of the year. After these are twelve others, one for each month, and there are those thousands who divide the days for a period of 360 days. Now here are the names of the four leaders for the four parts of the year: Milki'el, Hel'emmelek, Mel'ejal and Narel. Their leaders are Adnar'el, Ijasusa'el and Elome'el.

In the beginning of the year Mel'ejal rises first and rules, who is named also Tam'aini, the sun, and he rules for ninety-one days. He will bring sweat, heat and calms. All trees will grow leaves and those who produce fruit will do so. He is responsible for the corn crops, the abundance of roses and all flowers. The trees for the winter season will appear withered. Now he also has leaders responsible to him and they are Berka'el, Zelebs'el, and another, who heads a thousand others, called Hilujaseph.

[Some of these names have a meaning. Mel'ejal and Tam'aini both mean "the southern sun". Zelebs'el means "this is the heart of God".]

99

I spoke again to my son Methuselah and told him that I would tell him about my visions.

"Two visions appeared to me before I took a wife, one vision quite different from the other. The first vision came to me while I was learning to write, and the second before I married your mother. This was a terrible vision. Considering them both, I prayed to the Lord concerning them. I was at the time in the house of my grandfather, Mahalalel, when I saw in a vision how heaven collapsed and was taken and made to fall to the earth.

"As it fell to the earth, I saw how the earth was swallowed up into a great abyss and mountains were suspended on top of mountains, and I saw hills sink down low on other hills. High trees were pulled up like plants by their stems and hurled down and sank into the abyss.

"Then a word came into my mouth and I found myself crying aloud saying: 'The earth is destroyed!' My grandfather came to me and woke me up. 'Why did you cry out like that, my son? Why such a grief in your voice?' I told him all that I had seen in my vision and he answered me: 'A terrible thing you have obviously seen, my son. It appears to be regarding the sins of the world, and that it must face a great destruction. Now, my son, get up and pray to the Lord of Glory. As you are a believer, pray and ask that a part of the earth may remain and that He may not destroy the whole earth. For surely there will come from heaven a time of great destruction for the earth.'

"I did as he suggested and got up from my bed and went to pray to the Lord of Glory. I begged the Lord and besought Him in prayer. Then I got up and wrote down my prayer for future generations of the world. I will show you everything, Methuselah.

"Then I arose from there and found myself in a high place. I was in heaven and saw the sun rising in the east as the moon set in the west. There were a few stars and the whole earth set before me. Everything was as it had been when He created it in the beginning. I blessed the Lord and thanked Him for all He has created. Again I lifted up my hands in righteousness and blessed the Lord, the Holy One, and the Great One. I spoke, considering the wonderful creation of man, how we use our tongues of flesh. That flesh He made so we might speak, and the breath and the mouth by which we speak. All this we take for granted; all this He gave us in order that we may bless and glorify our God and heavenly king. For this we should all say as one voice:

Blessed be our Lord and King,
Great and mighty in your greatness,
Lord of the whole creation of heaven,
King of kings and God of the whole world.
Your power and kingship and greatness is for ever and ever,
And throughout all generations your dominion,
All the heavens, are your throne forever,
The whole earth's your footstool for ever and ever.
You have made and you shall rule over all things,
And nothing is impossible for you.
Wisdom is yours forever and abides and comes from you.
You know all things, nothing is kept from you; you know all secrets and hear everything; you see everything.

Some of the angels of heaven were guilty when they came to dwell in the flesh amongst mankind.
Even men shall be subject to your wrath until the great day of judgement.

Now, O God and Lord and Great King,
I implore and beseech you to fulfil my prayer,
To leave me a posterity on earth.
Not to destroy all the flesh of man, leaving the earth without inhabitants,
So that there shall be an eternal destruction.
Now, my Lord, destroy and take from the earth the flesh which has aroused your anger.
But the flesh of righteousness and uprightness established it as a plant of eternal seed.
Do not disregard this prayer of your servant, O Lord."

100

After this I had another dream, which I told my son: "Now listen to me, my son. Before I married your mother, Edna, I saw in a vision, whilst in bed, a bull coming from the earth, and it was white in colour. Behind it came a heifer, then two more bulls – one black, one red. Now the black bull gored the red one, chasing it across the earth until I could no longer see the red bull. The black bull grew and the heifer went to him and in time many oxen were born, who resembled the black bull and followed him wherever he travelled. Now the heifer was a cow and she went in search of the red bull but failed to find him and she was very sorrowful and sad at the loss. So sad was she that the black bull came to her and tried to console her and she was no longer sad. She bore a white bull and many other bulls and black cows.

"In my dream I saw the white bull grow up and become a great white bull, and in turn other white bulls were born, all resembling him. All of them sired white bulls in their likeness.

"After this I dreamt that I saw heaven above and a star fall from heaven and it got up from the earth and started to eat the pasture with the oxen. Then the coloured oxen came and changed places with one another and their pastures, and they lived with one another.

"I looked again up towards heaven and saw many stars coming down towards the earth to join that first star, and they took up the form of the bulls and lived amongst the cattle. Then I noticed that these stars, now in the form of bulls, covered the cows and they became pregnant. But instead of giving birth to heifers and bulls, the cows gave birth to asses, camels and elephants. This caused a lot of alarm amongst the oxen and they attacked these offspring and gored them with their horns and bit them. In return these creatures retaliated and attacked the oxen. All this brought terror upon the earth and the children of men ran from these creatures. I saw again how they began to gore and devour each other and the earth seemed to cry aloud.

"After this I raised my eyes to heaven where I saw in my dream, or vision, beings descending to earth like white men. There were four men and then, following them, came three more. These three came to me and grasped my hand and took me upwards to a high place and showed me a tower. It was high above the earth and all the hills were low. One of them spoke to me: 'Stay here and watch, for you will see everything that shall happen to these creatures, the elephants, camels and the asses, the stars and the oxen – all of them!'

"As I watched, one of the first of the four men seized the first star and bound it hand and foot and then cast it into an abyss that was both narrow and deep. It looked horrible and dark.

"One of the others drew a sword and gave it to the elephants, camels and the asses. With it they attacked one another, making the whole earth tremble. After this, one of the first four men gathered the fallen stars that had taken on animal form and stoned them and then bound them hand and foot and they were cast into that abyss of the earth.

"Now one of the four went to that first white bull and instructed him in secret so he would not be terrified. He had been born a white bull, but then became a man. He built for himself a great vessel to live in, and three bulls went to live with him in the vessel. It was then covered in.

"I looked again toward heaven and I saw a very high roof with seven water torrents flowing into an enclosure. In that great enclosure were fountains and the water began to rise until it engulfed the enclosure as the water overflowed and covered it. Now there was darkness and a mist arose above the water's surface. Within that enclosure were the cattle and they drowned in the rising water.

"As for the vessel, it floated on the water's surface and there remained up to the height of that mighty roof. Then the waters subsided and the chasms of the earth were levelled up and other abysses were opened to swallow up the water until the earth was revealed. The vessel eventually settled on the earth. Darkness withdrew and the light reappeared.

"Gradually, the man who once was the white bull came out of the vessel with the three bulls. One of the bulls was white, the other red as blood and the third black. The white bull departed from them."

101

"From that vessel came beasts of the field, birds and many animals: lions, tigers, wolves, dogs, hyenas, wild boars, foxes, squirrels, pigs, falcons, vultures, kites, eagles and ravens. Amongst these creatures there was the birth of a white bull. As they left the vessel they began to bite one another.

"The white bull that was born on the vessel bred with a wild ass. The wild asses multiplied. This white bull also sired a young bull and it in turn sired a wild black boar and a white sheep. From the black boar came many boars, but from the sheep came twelve others. When the twelve sheep had matured, one of the sheep was given up to the asses. These asses in turn gave that one sheep up to the wolves. They did not kill the sheep but it was allowed to live with them."

102

"The Lord brought the remaining eleven sheep to join the one sheep that lived amongst the wolves, and they began to multiply greatly in number. Now the wolves in turn began to fear the many flocks of sheep, and began to oppress them and destroy their offspring by casting them into the rivers. The sheep cried out loudly because of the deaths of their little ones, and their cries reached the Lord.

"A sheep was saved from amongst the wolves and escaped to live with the wild asses. I saw the other sheep how they lamented and cried out to the Lord. The lord of the sheep descended at the sound of the voices of the sheep and he came to them and lived with them in their pasture. He called that sheep which had escaped from the wolves, and he spoke with the sheep concerning the wolves. He told the sheep to go and warn the wolves not to touch the sheep. The sheep did as it was told by the Lord and went to the wolves. As it set out, another sheep met it and they went together to meet the wolves. They spoke to them and warned them not to touch the sheep again, as the Lord commanded. Yet the wolves continued to oppress the sheep with all their power and the sheep again cried out to the Lord.

"The Lord heard the cry of the sheep and came to them, and the sheep turned against the wolves and attacked them. It was now the turn of the wolves to cry and lament. Then the sheep became quiet and their crying ceased. I watched the sheep as they all departed from amongst the wolves, yet the eyes of the wolves were blinded and the wolves came after the sheep with all their might and power.

"Now the Lord went ahead of the sheep as their leader and all His sheep followed Him. They saw His face and it was dazzling and glorious and they were unable to look at Him. The wolves continued in their pursuit of the sheep and they caught up with the sheep as they reached the sea. Then the sea divided and the Lord led them through and placed Himself between the sheep and the wolves. The wolves continued to go after the sheep despite the parting of the waters, until they saw the Lord of the sheep. Then they turned to retreat but the sea closed in on them and swirled about and over them until they were drowned.

"As for the sheep, they left the sea for the wilderness, but there was neither grass nor water. Then I saw the Lord provide them with pasture and water and a sheep chosen to lead them. This sheep climbed a summit of rock. When the chosen sheep came down to the flock, the Lord was with him and the sheep saw the face of their Lord. His appearance was great and terrifying and very majestic, and they feared Him and their bodies trembled with fear. They cried out to their leader saying, 'We are not able to stand before our Lord or to look at Him.'

"The sheep that had led them climbed to the summit of the great rock. While he was away the other sheep wandered away, blinded to his words and the path he had shown them. This made the Lord of the sheep very angry. So the leader of the sheep went down to the flock and found many of them blinded and turning away from the path. When they saw him they trembled with fear and decided to return to the remainder of the flock who had remained faithful to the path. Those responsible for this turning away were killed. Then, seeing this, all the sheep became one flock again.

"In this vision I saw the sheep change into a man, who then built a house for the Lord. He then placed all the sheep into this house. Then the older, wiser sheep fell asleep [died]. All the little ones took the place of them that had gone and they all came to a new pasture and approached a stream of water. The man was still with them for a little longer, but then he withdrew from them and fell asleep [died]. They went to look for the man and when they found him they all cried bitterly. In due course they ceased their crying and went on, crossing the stream. I saw then that they chose two sheep leaders. They led the flock to a good place, a pleasant and glorious land. Then all the sheep were satisfied and they had a house built for the Lord.

"Now I saw that sometimes the eyes of these sheep were open, other times blinded. Then a sheep would arise from amongst them and lead them back to the right path and their eyes would again be opened.

"However, dogs and foxes and wild boars attacked those sheep and many were devoured. Then the Lord of the sheep raised up another sheep, a ram, from their midst. He led them and he did butt the dogs, foxes and wild boars until he had destroyed them all. Now the original leader of the sheep looked on at the ram and saw what it had done. It then gave up its own glory and attacked the very sheep it once led and its behaviour was seen by all. The Lord also saw what had been done and he sent the lamb to another lamb and it was raised to a ram and a new leader of the sheep. The new leader spoke to the lamb and it too became a prince amongst sheep. Yet during this time more dogs came to oppress the sheep. Now the first ram turned on the second and chased it from the flock. The first ram then became victim to the dogs.

"I then saw the second ram return and lead the little ones, and they grew to become adult sheep. The ram stood its ground against the dogs, foxes and wild boars that came to attack the flock. The ram protected the flock and fought off the wild beasts and killed them; the remainder escaped and left the sheep alone. In due course the ram had increased the flock but was of a great age and fell asleep.

"Then in the vision, a little sheep became a ram in the place of the old ram and became a prince. The house became great and broad, having been built for the sheep. There was also built a high tower on the house of the Lord. The Lord of the sheep stood on that tower and the sheep offered Him a full table.

"Alas, the sheep again went their own ways and forsook their house. Seeing this, the Lord sent sheep from amongst them to warn them, but the sheep turned on them and killed them, all but one, and that one sheep escaped and cried aloud over the sheep. They saw it and made plans to kill it, but the Lord saved it from the sheep and brought it up to be with Him. The Lord sent many other sheep to warn them, yet they ignored them and the Lord. They stopped going into the house of the Lord and were becoming blinded to the truth. The Lord brought much destruction to their belongings and their livelihood, but they still betrayed Him. Such was the anger of the Lord that he gave them over to lions, tigers, wolves and hyenas. Even into the hands of foxes and all wild beasts. And these tore them apart.

"Seeing this troubled me and I cried out to the Lord and appealed to Him with regard to the plight of the sheep. He remained unmoved, although he saw all that took place on the earth and appeared to rejoice in the destruction. But then He called seventy shepherds and gave the sheep over to their keeping in their own pastures. The Lord told them they would obey His every command. To kill them whom He wishes to be removed from the earth. Then the shepherds took the sheep allocated to them by the Lord and killed those sheep, as the Lord had demanded.

"Whilst this was taking place, the Lord called another and spoke to him: 'Observe and mark everything that the shepherds will do to those sheep, for they will destroy more of them than I commanded them to kill. Record all excesses of each shepherd as to the number of sheep they kill which I have not commanded them to kill. Then return to Me and tell the number of the sheep they destroyed and how many they had given to others to destroy. I shall use this as a testimony against them, for I shall know every deed they do. I will comprehend their actions and shall see all they do, whether or not by my command. They will not know this and you will not tell them! You will say nothing to them about their wrongs.'

"Now the seventy shepherds carried out the killings and killed more than the Lord had commanded. Others they delivered to be killed by lions. The lions and the tigers ate the sheep and also shared the sheep with wild boars. They went and destroyed the house built for the sheep, and the tower of the Lord.

"I watched in complete sorrow as this all took place. All that the seventy shepherds did was recorded in a book, day by day. Then the book was taken up before the face of the Lord and read out aloud, the whole account. Then the Lord took the book and read what had been written. The Lord then sealed the book and laid it down.

"As for the shepherds, they pastured the sheep for twelve hours. Then I saw three sheep leave the pasture and return to the ruins of the house. They then started to rebuild it, but wild boars started to hinder them but with little success. They worked hard and rebuilt the house and the tower. They laid a table before the tower but the bread they used was polluted. The eyes of the other sheep were again blinded, but so were the shepherds' eyes. The blinded sheep delivered these few sheep up for destruction by the shepherds and they were trampled down and killed.

"I looked at the Lord, but He seemed unmoved by all this, even when the shepherds gave the sheep up to the wild beasts to devour. Again, all this was recorded in a book, which, as before, was taken up to the Lord and read out. The Lord took the book and set it beside Him and departed.

"Now I saw in my vision all the birds of heaven coming, being led by eagles. There were eagles, ravens, vultures and kites. They descended on the flocks of sheep and started to pick at their eyes and to devour their flesh. The sheep cried out in vain for the shepherd, but he never came to them and few remained alive.

"To those remaining white sheep lambs were born, and they cried out but the sheep ignored them and seemed oblivious to their existence. Ravens saw the lambs and flew at them and took one of the lambs away to devour it. A little while later these lambs had small horns developing on their heads and the ravens struck at the horns until they fell to the ground, all but one – to this one young sheep there developed a great horn. As soon as it had grown to its full size the sheep in the pasture had their eyes opened. The sheep and the rams saw the young sheep with open eyes and the rams ran to its side.

"The birds still continued to attack the sheep and they remained silent, but not the rams – they cried out and saw the ravens attack the young sheep with the great horn. Despite their attacks on the young sheep, they found they had no power over it. The shepherds, eagles, vultures and kites also saw the ravens fail. So they came together as one group and met the ravens. They all agreed that between them they would attack the great horned sheep and destroy the horn. Even the other sheep joined them. Then the young sheep with the great horn was seen as a ram and it cried out for help. Then a sword was given to the young sheep and it turned and attacked the birds and all the beasts in that field and they all fled.

"I then saw the man in heaven with the book, he who recorded everything the shepherds did. He wrote down the names of the shepherds and carried the book up to the Lord. The record showed that these shepherds had caused much destruction, more than the previous shepherds had done.

"The wrath of the Lord was great and He came down to the shepherds with a staff in His hand and He struck at the ground. The ground opened and the beasts and the birds fell into the hole in the earth and it appeared to swallow them.

"In that pleasant land the Lord sat on a throne that had been erected for Him and He picked up those sealed books. Then the Lord called those first seven shepherds, the first white ones. He commanded that they bring to Him, beginning with the first star that had led the way, all the stars with male members like those of horses. They did as He commanded. The Lord turned to the man who recorded the deeds of the shepherds: 'Take those seventy shepherds who I gave the sheep to, who in turn killed more than I told them to.' They were taken and bound and brought before the Lord. The Lord then judged the stars; they were found guilty and were sent to the place of condemnation, a place full of fire and burning pillars of flame. Then the seventy shepherds were also judged and found guilty and they too were taken away and thrown into an abyss of fire. As for the sheep that remained blinded, they too were judged and found guilty and cast into the same fiery abyss and they were burned both flesh and bone.

"The abyss was in an old house, to its right hand side. When all this had taken place, I saw the whole house fold up. All the pillars of the house, the ornaments and beams, all of it was taken away and replaced to the south of the land.

"I then saw the Lord provide a new house in the place of the old one. It was greater and higher than the original. All the pillars were new and so were the ornaments to go inside the new house. The sheep were now inside this new house. Then all the beasts of the field and the birds crept back and paid homage to the sheep inside the house, making petitions and obeying the sheep."

103

"The three who were clothed in white, those that brought me by the hand, held my hand again, but so did that ram with the great horn. They all took me up and sat me down in the midst of those sheep, before the judgement took place. These sheep were all white, their wool abundant and clean. There sat the Lord also and with them were the beasts and the birds who had come to repent the wrong they had done. The Lord was greatly pleased by their repentance and there was great rejoicing in the house. The sheep produced the sword which had been given to them; this they placed before the Lord. It was sealed before the face of the Lord. All were invited into the house although it was not big enough to house them all.

"I then saw the birth of a white bull with large horns. All the beasts of the field and all the birds feared him, so they made petitions toward him all the time. I then saw all their generations become transformed and they all became white bulls. Yet the first amongst them became a lamb; this in turn became a great animal with great black horns. The Lord was pleased with it and with all the oxen. I fell asleep after this and had another vision."

104

"I awoke and praised and blessed the name of the Lord, our God. Then I was overcome with weeping and I cried on account of what I had seen, for everything shall come to be fulfilled. All the deeds of men in the order of things were shown to me. The visions I had seen troubled me deeply in my heart."

105

[Enoch wrote this as a doctrine of wisdom that has been praised by men as a judgement for the world. This is also written for future generations who observe "uprightness and peace".]

> Let not your spirit be troubled on account of the times in which you live. The Holy and Great One has appointed days for all things.
>
> The righteous shall arise from their sleep and they will walk in the paths of righteousness. Their conversations and their path in this life shall be in eternal goodness and grace.
>
> The Lord will be gracious to the righteous and give them eternal uprightness; He will give them power so that they shall be endowed with goodness and righteousness. They shall walk in eternal light.
>
> Sin shall perish in darkness forever and shall no more be seen from that appointed day, for evermore.

I then spoke to my son Methuselah and asked him to call the family together, as the Word calls me and the spirit is poured out upon me. I told him that I shall show him everything that shall happen to him, now and forever.

He called them to him and brought the family to me, and I spoke to them and said, "Hear me, all of you, my words, and pay attention to what I have to say. Love uprightness and walk in the truth. Do not have a double heart nor associate with those who have a double heart. Walk always in righteousness and let it guide you on the paths of goodness. Let righteousness be your companion. For I know that violence must increase on the earth and a great chastisement will be executed on the earth. Then all unrighteousness shall come to an end. It will be destroyed!

"All unrighteousness shall again be consummated on the earth, along with deeds of unrighteousness and deeds of violence. Transgression shall prevail in a twofold degree. Sin, unrighteousness, blasphemy and violence of all kinds, to varying degrees, will increase; so will apostasy, transgressions and uncleanness also increase.

"Then shall come the great chastisement from heaven above and our Holy Lord will come forth with wrath and chastisement and He shall execute judgement on the whole world. In those days violence shall be cut off like a plant from its roots and the roots of such unrighteousness, together with deceit, shall be destroyed from under heaven.

"All idols of worship belonging to the heathen will be abandoned. Their temples burned with fire and they will be removed from the whole earth. Such heathen shall be cast into the fire of judgement and they will perish in wrath and grievous judgement forever. Then the righteous shall rise from their sleep and wisdom shall be given to every one of them forever. As for sinners, the sword shall destroy them. They will be cut off from the blasphemers in every place, along with those who have planned violence. These also will perish by the sword.

"Now listen to me and let me show you the paths of righteousness and the paths of violence. I will show them again to you so that you recognise them and understand what will take place. Walk always in the paths of righteousness not in the paths of violence. For whoever walks in the paths of unrighteousness shall perish for ever."

106

I passed the books to my son and the family and continued to speak to them: "Now, concerning the children of righteousness and the elect of the world, the very plant of uprightness, all this I shall speak to you about. According to that which appeared to me in my heavenly vision and through the word of His holy angels and from heavenly writings.

"I shall start at the beginning of my life on earth. I was born on the seventh, the first week of the year, during a period where judgement and righteousness still endured. After me, in the second week, there will arise great wickedness. Deceit shall have sprung up but there shall be the first end and a man shall be saved. Then after this period is ended, unrighteousness shall rise up and a law will be introduced for sinners.

"The third week shall come and go and at its close a man shall be elected as the plant of righteous judgement. His prosperity shall become the plant of righteousness for evermore.

"The fourth week shall come, and at its close, there will be visions of the holy and righteous. Again there will be a law for all generations and an enclosure shall be made for them.

"The fifth week will come and close and the house of glory and dominion shall be built forever. Then after the sixth week all that live at that time will be blinded, for they will forsake wisdom and accept godlessness.

"Now a man shall ascend in that week and at its close the house of dominion will be set alight and will be burnt. The whole race of the chosen ones will be dispersed. In the seventh week an apostate generation will arise and they will undertake many apostate deeds [abandonment of loyalty and religious faith]. At the close of this period shall there be elected those of righteousness who will receive a sevenfold instruction concerning all His creation. Yet who is there from among mankind who are able to hear and bear the voice of the Holy One without being troubled? Who can behold all the works of heaven and have understanding of the things of heaven, to see a soul or a spirit and tell others of what has been seen regarding their end? Who is there who, at this time, can know the length and breadth of the whole earth and give account of how it has been measured? Who is there who can state the size of heaven itself and the very highest of heaven, even the size and depths of the universe?

"Then shall come the eighth week, a week of righteousness. It shall bear the sword of righteous judgement that it be used against the oppressors and sinners, all being delivered into the hands of the righteous ones. At its close there will be houses given to the righteous. One house shall be built for the Great King and filled with glory for evermore. All mankind shall take to the paths of uprightness, even to the ninth week, where righteous judgement shall be revealed to the whole world. Then all the works of the godless shall vanish from across the earth. The world itself shall be written down for destruction.

"After this will be the tenth week in a seventh part, a time of great eternal judgement in which He, the Lord, will execute vengeance amongst His angels. A great change will affect heaven as the first part of heaven will depart and pass away, but a new heaven shall appear and all the powers of heaven shall give sevenfold light. From that moment on there will be many weeks without number, even forever [the period known as the Apocalypse of Weeks]. All will dwell in goodness and righteousness, and sin shall be no more. The very word will cease to exist forever."

107

"And now I say to you all, love righteousness and walk in its paths, for such ways are acceptable, but the paths of unrighteousness will lead to destruction and will vanish. Certain men of a particular generation shall see paths of violence and death but they will not follow these paths.

"Now I say to you who are righteous, keep away from the paths of wickedness and death, or else you will be destroyed. Seek therefore the right paths and an elect life that leads to peace, that you shall live and prosper. Keep hold of my words; keep them safe in your heart. Know that sinners will come and tempt all men to evilly entreat wisdom so no place be found for her. For no temptation will diminish.

"Those who build upon unrighteousness, oppression and deceit shall be suddenly overthrown and by the sword they shall die. Also, they who gather up gold and silver, in judgement shall perish. Therefore, you rich who have put your trust in your many riches, these will be taken from you because you have failed to consider the Most High God because of your riches.

"Beware also those who have blasphemed and been unrighteous, for you are now ready for the day of slaughter, the day of darkness and great judgement. For He that has created you will overthrow you and there will be no compassion. He will rejoice at your destruction! In those days the righteous ones shall be a reproach to sinners and the godless."

108

"Oh, that my eyes were but a cloud of water that I may weep over you all, that my tears come down as like water so that I might rest from my troubled heart! For who has permitted you to practise reproaches and wickedness? Remember that judgement will overtake you, you sinners!

"As for you who are righteous, do not be fearful, for again the Lord will deliver you out of the hands of the evil ones. For the Lord will allow you to execute judgement upon them as you will.

"Beware those of you who criticise and denounce, who despise and curse that which cannot be reversed, for such cannot be healed because of their sins. Also those who retaliate against their neighbour with evil intentions, for they too shall receive retaliation according to their actions. For those of you who are lying witnesses and who do an injustice, all shall suddenly perish.

"As for all sinners who have persecuted the righteous, they will be given up and shall receive persecution in return for their injustice. The burden they shall bear will be heavy indeed."

109

"I want you to be hopeful, all those of you who are righteous. Remember that all sinners will perish from before your eyes. You will exercise lordship over them according to your desires.

"In the Great Day of Tribulation, when sinners shall be judged, your children shall rise up as eagles. Higher than even the vultures shall be your abode. Then they will descend and enter the crevices of the earth and the clefts of the rock before the face of the unrighteous, forever. There shall be sirens that sigh because of them, and they will weep. For you who have suffered, have no fear, for you will be healed and a bright light shall cover you and the heavenly voice of rest you will hear.

"Now, you sinners! You who have riches that make you appear like the righteous, your very hearts will convict you as sinners and this shall act as a testimony against you and as a memorial to your evil deeds. Those of you who have eaten of the best foods and drunk the best wines, you who have looked down on the poor and the lowly with your pride and might and arrogance, you will come to drink at many fountains. Once this is done you will wither away, for you have forsaken the true fountain, the Fountain of Life.

"Then to those who have worked unrighteousness, spoken blasphemy and deceit, such shall be your memorial! As for you who consider yourselves mighty, who have oppressed the righteous, the day of your destruction is coming. You shall see many good days come to the righteous whom you oppressed."

110

"Rest assured, my righteous ones, that shame will come upon all sinners and they will perish on the day of judgement. Be assured, therefore, that the Most High is mindful of their destruction.

"You, sinners! What are you going to do? Where do you think you are going to run to, to escape on that fateful day of judgement? Do you expect the Lord to listen to your prayers? For He will only listen to the prayers of the righteous!

"He will say to you: 'You have been companions of sinners!' How will you be able to deny it? For His ears are only inclined to the righteous and only their prayers will reach Him. For the words and deeds of sinners will be read out before the Great Holy One. The faces of sinners will be covered with shame. He will come to reject every action and works that have been grounded on unrighteousness. Even those sinners who live on the sea will not escape.

"Those of you who have acquired silver and gold through unrighteous means will say, 'We have become rich and have possessions, having been able to acquire everything we have ever desired and much more. Let us do as we desire. We gathered silver and all good things and our homes abound with many things. Our larders are full of food and our cellars full of wine.' For these people, their very lies shall flow away like water and their riches shall escape them and they will become subject to a great curse at the end of their lives."

111

This is important, so I swear, so listen to me both wise and foolish of the earth. You will all have many experiences on earth in your lifetime and you will come to see men putting on more adornments than a woman, more coloured garments than a virgin. In royalty and in grandeur as in power, dressed in silver, gold and purple. In such splendour and with such fine food they shall have in abundance as though it was all mere water. Yet they will be poor in doctrine and wisdom and in the end shall perish together with all their possessions. They will lose all their splendour and glory, in their shame and in their slaughter. They will come to great destitution and their spirits will be cast into a furnace of fire.

"I swear to you sinners, as a mountain has not become a slave and a hill a handmaiden, sin was not sent to the earth. Man created sin himself and under a great curse many shall fall who commit it. As barrenness has not been given to a woman, yet through her own deeds and lifestyle she dies childless.

"Again, I swear to you sinners, by the Holy Great God, that all your evil deeds will be revealed in heaven, especially deeds of oppression, for nothing is hidden from the Lord. Do not make the excuse that you do not see every sin you have committed or that you had no idea your deeds were being recorded in heaven, for the Lord sees all things! Everything is recorded from the day you were born up to the day of your judgement.

"You foolish ones! For through your folly shall you perish. For your deeds against the wise you will be taken to task. Do not expect to live, for you are being prepared for the day of destruction. You have refused the ransom – indeed, you do not know of such a ransom paid for your lives.

"As for you who are obstinate of heart, you have worked wickedness and spilled blood in your pursuit of good things to eat and drink. You fill your bodies at the expense of others. The Lord placed all good things on the earth in abundance, but you have had more than your share and therefore you will never know peace of mind. Many of you have loved the deeds of unrighteousness, yet you think you deserve good fortune and happiness for yourselves, do you not? Consider this carefully: you will be delivered into the hands of the righteous, who will show you no mercy, for they will destroy you!

"You who have enjoyed the tribulation of others, you who have actually rejoiced in their demise, you will never even have a grave of your own. As for those of you who have contradicted the words of the righteous, for you there is no hope of life.

"There are many that write down lying words and godless writing. They have written down their own lies that those who read them may come to accept them as truth, acting according to falsehood, even bringing death upon their neighbours. Such people will die suddenly.

"Listen carefully and read my words, you who work godlessness, who glory in lying, who even extol such lies. You will never know a truly happy life, but will perish. Many pervert the truth and transgress God's eternal law, making themselves into what they are not – that is living a lie! You all will be trodden down underfoot by men.

"Now, as for the righteous among you, make ready to raise your prayers and praise and to be a testimony before angels. For they will place the sin of sinners before the Most High as a memorial. The time will come when every nation of the world will be stirred up and the families of all nations will arise on the day of destruction. In that day the destitute will carry off their children to a place where they will abandon them to perish in time. Even the newborn will be left alone by their mothers, left to die. Such parents will have no pity at all on their loved ones.

"Again, at that time sinners will face a time of bloodshed. For all who worship idols and images of stone, gold, silver and wood, clay and all kinds of materials, for they worship with impure spirits and demons will be in them. Others will become godless by reason of their folly from within their hearts and they shall be as though blind because of what is in their hearts. They will become fearful through visions when they are asleep. Because they shall become godless they will be fearful, for all they have gained has been through lies. Their worship of stone shall bring about instant death.

"I will tell you this, my blessed ones: accept the words of wisdom and understand them. Observe the words and the paths set for you by the Most High God; walk in the path of His righteousness.

"Those who spread evil to their neighbours shall be slain in Hell. Be careful all of you who make deceitful and false claims, giving false measure rather than what is owed to another. To you who cause bitterness on the earth, you will be utterly consumed. A warning now to you landowners who have fooled many through grievous toil to build you houses, for through this every brick and stone and wood used, each piece of building material, becomes a sin. I warn you: you will never have any peace.

"There are many in this world that have rejected their heritage, the heritage of their fathers and the good measure they had inherited, for some false doctrine of idol worship. For they shall have no rest.

"Those in this world who work unrighteousness and help to oppress the poor, who across the nations will kill their neighbours until the time of great judgement, will answer to the Lord. He shall cast down your glory and afflict your hearts, for you have aroused His fierce indignation. You will be destroyed with the sword. All the holy and righteous shall remember your evil deeds and sins."

112

"In those days to come, fathers and their sons will meet at an appointed place, where they shall all be attacked. Brother with brother shall they die and streams will flow with their blood. For there, fathers kills their sons and their sons will kill their sons in turn. For these sinners will kill one another. So many will lie dead in that place with spilled blood that a horse will be up to its chest in the blood of sinners. All types of vehicle will be submerged to their very height in blood.

"Now angels will descend from heaven into secret places on the earth. For those who are responsible for bringing sin will be gathered together. Then the Lord Most High will rise up on that day of judgement to bring great judgement on all sinners. Over all the righteous and holy He will appoint guardians from amongst His holy angels. They will guard these righteous and holy ones, as the Lord regards them as the 'apple of His eye', until such time as He brings to an end all manner of wickedness and sin.

"Whilst this takes place the righteous and the holy will enter a sleep, for they have nothing more to fear. Those on the earth shall see these righteous and holy ones asleep in His security. They shall then see and understand the words of the book, recognising that their riches cannot save them as their sins overthrow them. So now, sinners of the world, beware of the impending day of anguish; you who through the centuries have afflicted the righteous and burnt them at the stake, and in other ways, you killed them. You will be judged by your deeds in this world. For those obstinate of heart that watched evil ways and devised wickedness, you will be filled with a great fear. You will look for help, but there are none to help you.

"As for those of you who have lied and spoken evil from your heart and mouth, you will be taken to task because of this and the works you have done with your hands. You brought godlessness into the world. For you are bound for hell and you will be burnt, a burning far worse than any earthly fire you have experienced.

"Some of you have judged whilst being in the world. Your deeds in your lifetime will be enquired of you, that you will be judged according to the judgement you meted out to others. Even the sun, moon and stars will testify to your every deed and sin. The very mist and clouds have recorded your actions and deeds. For all living things and the very elements will know of your sins. The very harshness of frost and snow and all manner of plagues will come upon you and you will not be able to withstand them."

113

"Observe heaven, children of heaven, and see every area of God's work and fear Him, for nothing He does is wrong. If He withholds the rain and the dew, what can you do about it? If He sends His anger down on you, how can you beg Him for mercy because of the way you spoke to Him? You used proud and insolent words against His righteousness. How can you expect to have peace? Have you never seen sailors on board a ship in a terrible storm? Have they not feared for their personal possessions as much as for their own miserable lives? Are not the seas and oceans and all their movements and tides the works of God? Has he not preset limits to the doings of seas and oceans? Confining the seas and oceans by way of sands and land? Consider this: at His reproof an entire sea could dry up, causing all its fish and creatures to die, yet you sinners do not respect or love Him, let alone fear His might!

Has God not made heaven and earth and all that has been created therein? Who has given understanding and wisdom to everything that moves on the earth and the sea below? The sailors fear the sea, but sinners fear not the Lord our God!"

114

"In those days to come, He will bring upon you a terrible fire, but where are you to run to? When the Lord sends His word against you, will you not be full of fear? Even the luminaries in the universe will be filled with fear. As for the earth, it will tremble and all will be alarmed.

"Then the commands given to the angels shall commence, but even they will hide themselves from the presence of the Great Glory of God. All the children of earth shall also be trembling with fear. For all sinners will be under a curse forever and shall know no peace.

"Yet the righteous amongst you need not fear but should live in hope and the knowledge that you will die in righteousness. Be not alarmed should your spirit descend to the place of the dead. Remember that in your earthly life your body did not exist according to your goodness. Wait there for the day of judgement, the day of cursing and chastisement.

"At the moment of your death sinners will look down on you and say, 'Look – as we die, so do the righteous. What benefits do they reap for all their good deeds? For they even died in grief and in darkness, as we shall do. What more have they got that we have not had also? So therefore we are all equal, for they receive as much or as little as we do. What will they see which is different to us, in the end? Where is the light for them to see they are in darkness as well!'

"If this is so, listen to me, sinners! You have been content to eat and drink, to rob and to steal, and sin is in your every thought. Many of you have stripped many of the belongings of the righteous and you have taken and acquired much wealth through these means, and you say you see good days. Have you not considered how the righteous live? They have not committed any violence, not even to the time of their death, yet you insist that they perish and that they will share the same fate as you will after you're dead!"

115

"Listen to me again! I swear to you, the righteous, by the glory of the Great and Honoured Mighty One, by His greatness I know a mystery and have read heavenly words in the holy books, finding written there that all goodness and joy and glory are prepared for them. This has been written for the spirits of those who have died in righteousness: that manifold good shall be given to you the righteous in recompense for your labours, for your lot is abundantly greater than that of the living. After death you as spirits shall live and rejoice. Your spirits will not perish, nor shall the Lord forget you.

"As for sinners, when you have died, if you die in the wealth of your sins and many say, 'Blessed are sinners: they have seen all their days. They have died in prosperity and in their wealth. They have not seen any troubles or been involved in murder in their life, therefore they die in honour. For no judgement has taken place against them.' This they say, as they wish not to speak ill of the dead, then consider this carefully: you must come to understand that their spirits will descend to hell to great tribulation, into a darkness, their sins as chains, and there they will encounter a burning flame, where there is to be grievous judgement. This judgement shall continue for all the generations of the world. They shall not encounter any peace.

"Now I ask you not to disregard the righteous, the good people who are in this life. Listen to what they have said: 'In our troubled days we have worked hard and experienced every trouble, met with evil and been almost consumed by its efforts. We have become few over generations and our spirit appears small. Many of us have been destroyed. Others have found no help. Not even a kind word came our way! There have been times when we have been tortured and even hoped that another day would never come. There have been those of us who had expected to be the head but became the tail. We have worked and toiled but often our toil has not paid off; there has been no satisfaction. Throughout the centuries we have been made to be food for sinners and the unrighteous and they have laid heavy burdens upon us all. We have been hated, and we have been struck. Despite lowering our heads and necks in humility, they have still hated us and have shown no pity towards us. Although many of us have tried to escape to a place of safety and peacefulness, there has been no such place on earth.

"'Many times through our life on earth we have complained to those who govern us. We cried out for justice against those who persecuted us, but they have always ignored our petitions and would not listen to us. In fact, they in high places assisted our persecutors and those who rob us and kill us. They want to remove many of us from the earth, to reduce our number. The rulers and governments of the people concealed their oppression from the eyes of the world but did nothing to relieve the burdens others put us under. They prefer to ignore us and refuse to acknowledge our pleas to them.'"

116

"Again I swear to you that in heaven the angels will remember you for the good you have done, before the glory of the Great One. For your names are written, and they are known by the Lord your God.

"Be ever hopeful: even if you are afflicted and put to shame for your faith in the Lord, you shall shine like the lights of heaven. You will shine and you will be seen. All the portals of heaven shall be opened to you. If you cry for judgement it shall appear to you. For all your trials and tribulations on earth shall come upon those who afflicted you on earth, even rulers and governments. Do not lose hope! Hold on to it, and you shall have great joy, as do the angels in heaven.

"On that great day of judgement you will have no need to hide, for you will not appear as sinners do, for you will escape the great judgement of all the generations of the world. Fear not, you who are righteous in the sight of the Lord. When you see sinners growing strong and prospering in many ways, keep away from their violent ways. Remember, you are to become companions of the hosts of heaven.

"Many sinners say to themselves, 'All our sins will not be found out nor written down!' This is untrue, for all sins are recorded against every sinner. Be they committed in the day or at night, the day sees and the night records. So do not be godless in your heart. Do not lie or alter words of truth. Never accuse the Lord your God with telling lies, for you would be committing a great sin!

"Yes, sinners and the godless will alter words, they will pervert the truth in so many ways, some very craftily. They will speak wicked words, lie and practise great deceits. They will write books concerning the truth and will twist the words for their own benefit. When they do write down truthfully, their language can change the truth through faulty translations. Worry not, for there will be books handed down and given to the righteous and the wise and they will believe in them. These books will bring both joy and righteousness and much wisdom. What they shall learn from these books will lead them to a rightful path, and they will find recompense from their learning."

117

"In those days to come, the Lord will summon the children of the earth to testify concerning their wisdom. Show them, for you are their guides and recompense over the whole world. For the Lord has said: 'I and My Son will be united with them forever in the paths of righteousness throughout their lives. You all will have peace. Therefore, rejoice, you children of the righteous! Amen!'"

118

I wrote another book for my son Methuselah, to be read by those who come after him who keep the Law of God until that last day. For all that have done good shall wait for those days, until an end is made of those who do evil in the world, when sin will pass away. For their names will be deleted from the Book of Life and from the Holy Books. The seed of sinners will be destroyed forever. Their very spirits will be destroyed. Within a chaotic wilderness their cries will be heard and there will be a fire into which they will enter and burn. It is a place where the earth does not exist.

I saw there a cloud, almost invisible. It was impossible to look over the top of it. Then I saw a flame burning brightly and things like shining mountains circling to and fro. By my side was an angel and I asked the angel what was this bright shining thing, and whose voice was heard coming from it, crying in pain. The angel told me that this place was where the spirits of sinners were thrown – those who sinned, blasphemed, and those who did evil deeds; those who perverted everything that the Lord has ever spoken through His prophets and even the words He will speak in the future. For some of these are written down in order that the angels may read and know what will happen to each sinner, even the spirits of the humble, those who have afflicted bodies, and those recompensed by God. This also included those who have been put to shame by wicked men.

There are those who have never loved gold, silver or any of the good things in the world, but who have even given their bodies to be tortured for the love of God. These are they who, since they were born, did not lust after earthly food but lived according to the word of the Lord. Although for their faith they were tried by the Lord often, they never wavered and their spirits were seen to be pure. It was they who stood fast amid trials and tribulations and still they blessed the Lord.

The Lord will recompense them for their love for the Lord, and for heaven, which was more than their love for their earthly life. Despite being trodden down by wicked and resentful men, despite experiencing abuse and reviling and, in some cases, being put to shame, they always blessed and had faith in the Lord.

The Lord said, "Now I will summon the spirits of the good who belong to the generation of light. I will transform those who were born in darkness, who in the flesh were not recompensed with such honour as their faithfulness deserves. For I will bring forth in shining light those who have loved My holy name. Each will sit upon a throne of honour and shall be resplendent forever. Righteousness is the judgement of God. As for the faithful, they shall receive faithfulness in the habitation of the upright paths. For they will see those who were born in darkness and who have been led into darkness, while the righteous shall be resplendent. All sinners shall see them resplendent and indeed shall go where days and seasons are prescribed for them."

AUTHOR'S NOTE

The Letter of St Jude verses 14–16 speaks about Enoch:

"It was also about these things that Enoch, in the seventh generation from Adam, prophesied. Saying, 'See, the Lord is coming with ten thousands of His holy ones, to execute judgement on all, and to convict every one of all the deeds of the ungodliness that they have committed in such an ungodly way. And all the harsh things that ungodly sinners have spoken against Him.' These are grumblers and malcontents; they indulge their own lusts; they are bombastic in speech, flattering people to their own advantage."

[From the New Revised Standard Version of the Bible.]